GROWING UP WITH CRICKET

GROWING UP WITH CRICKET

Some Memories of a Sporting Education

ALAN GIBSON

London
GEORGE ALLEN & UNWIN
Boston   Sydney

George Allen & Unwin (Publishers) Ltd,
40 Museum Street, London WC1A 1LU, UK

George Allen & Unwin (Publishers) Ltd,
Park Lane, Hemel Hempstead, Herts HP2 4TE, UK

Allen & Unwin Inc.,
Fifty Cross Street, Winchester, Mass 01890, USA

George Allen & Unwin Australia Pty Ltd,
8 Napier Street, North Sydney, NSW 2060, Australia

First published in 1985

British Library Cataloguing in Publication Data

Gibson, Alan, *1923–*
    Growing up with cricket: some memories of a
sporting education.
1. Cricket – Anecdotes, facetiae, satire, etc.
I. Title
796.35'8   GV919
ISBN 0–04–796099–X

Set in 11 on 13 point Garamond by Nene Phototypesetters Ltd, Northampton
and printed in Great Britain by Butler & Tanner Ltd, Frome and London

To

The Sage of Longparish

Who is the best cricket writer of my generation and one of the best friends I have ever made through a game which has produced many

Contents

Introduction

Cricket has played a large part in my life, though it has remained separate from most of the rest of it. Some years ago, I wrote an autobiography about the things which seemed to me most important, and cricket did not come into it much. Yet I knew that cricket *was* important to me, in a different kind of way, and had a feeling that I might write of my cricketing experiences later on. Here is an attempt to do so. It is not a cricketing autobiography, but it gives some account of my associations with the game, especially my earlier associations. As I seek to explain, it took me a long time to take it sensibly, to grow up with it. I used to get far too worked up about it. I judge that it was only about 1955, upon the re-tirement of Hutton, that my views upon cricket were of any value at all. After that, much more by accident than design, I found myself becoming a regular broadcaster and writer upon the game, and it was certainly a blessing for my listeners and readers that I had gradually lost that partisan passion. I have not written much in this book about the last quarter of a century (except when reminiscence has occasionally drawn my thoughts forward). I have written all too much about recent times already, and there is no point in vain repetition. But I thought I would like to set down some account of those earlier cricketing years, those earlier cricketers and those earlier frenzies and furies, because although rather ashamed of them I do privately relish them. I warn you that you will find little here about the more modern characters – men such as Boycott and Lillee – and their inflammatory sagas. I find myself bored with them. Should I live long enough, I might one day gain some perspective upon them, and write another book called 'Growing Old with Cricket'.

Some passages of this book, though usually amended, have appeared in newspapers and magazines before, though none I think in a hard cover. Where I am quoting directly I indicate it in the text. But it is essentially a new book, which I have spent several years putting together, planing to its theme and, I hope, making it acceptable. Damn it, I am getting too humble: it is a poor pedlar who begins by apologising for his own bundle of goods. I can at least assure you that the book is written by the man whose name appears on the cover, which is comparatively rare in the modern profusion of cricket books. This is not to say that I have not had my share of 'ghosts', some of whom may whisper in these pages.

High Littleton, 1984 ALAN GIBSON

I

A Yorkshire Cockney

'Shake a bridle over a Yorkshireman's grave,
and he will rise up and steal a horse'
*Old north country saying,
probably Lancastrian in origin*

Although I have lived most of my life in the west of England, and ask nowhere better to live, I was born in Yorkshire, in Sheffield, only a mile or two from Bramall Lane. This had much to do with my early affection for cricket, which has lasted for a long time. Not that I remember anything of Sheffield, from the time I lived there, though I have often revisited it. When I was two years old, my father, who was a Baptist minister, moved to Ilkley. There was a fine cricket ground at Ilkley. A young man called Frank Smailes was winning a reputation there, and bound to play for the county soon, everybody said. All the talk in the summer was of cricket. At the end of morning service, as we gathered by the doors for a chat – it was the happiest twenty minutes of the day for me, because kind old ladies would give me small delicious sweets called dewdrops – my father's sermon was less discussed than how Yorkshire were doing. The biggest stir I can remember in that pleasant town was when Herbert Sutcliffe came to play in a match there.

After five years at Ilkley we moved to Leyton in East London. This was not a happy change for a small boy who had grown used to the country, but there was a compensation: our house overlooked the Essex County Cricket Ground. I must have seen something of nearly every match played there in the next four seasons, until

Essex gave up the ground (though in latter years they have returned to it for a week a season) and began their nomadic life. Ilkley and Leyton: this was my grounding in the game, and at Leyton I began to see the great players, not understanding them, but glimpsing in a childlike way their genius.

Clearly I can recall Hobbs: his appearance, rather than his batting. One Saturday, Essex had batted for most of the day, with some success, and Surrey went in at about six o'clock. We small boys, and many of our elders too, went out on to the ground, and formed an applauding lane for Hobbs and Sandham as they came out. It was not a tumultuous applause but a reverent one. The only other opening pair accorded this tribute at Leyton was Holmes and Sutcliffe.

Clearly I can recall Larwood in action. It must have been about 1932, when he was at his brief but awe-inspiring peak. It was years later that I read the much used term 'carpet-slippered' to describe Larwood's run-up, but as soon as I did, memory clicked. He did not take a long run, but took it fast with a perfect rhythm. We trembled as he approached our beloved Essex batsmen. I remember that once D. R. Wilcox hit him for seven (three runs and four overthrows). Wilcox was a young man, still an undergraduate, a pretty good player. He was the first man I ever saw wearing a Cambridge cap, which was an added joy, because in those days I was an ardent Cambridge supporter (in the East End in those days you had to be either Oxford or Cambridge, especially at Boat Race time). I wonder if anyone else ever hit Larwood for seven.

I have a recollection of Hammond at Leyton. He batted for a long time one afternoon, but no, I did not remember his style or splendour: I remembered that he wore a peculiar grey floppy hat, something like a trilby rescued from a dustbin. I was not drawn to Hammond. The hat seemed to add insult to injury.

You must realise that at this time I was fiercely partisan. I never forgot that I was a Yorkshireman, but Essex was my home side, and I always supported Essex, except when they played Yorkshire. I had not reached the stage when I could admire a cricketer simply for his skill, if he was on the wrong side.

I did, though, enjoy a big innings, over 200, played for the New Zealanders by C. S. Dempster in 1931. The New Zealanders were not championship competitors, and so we could afford to feel sympathetic towards them. I also enjoyed watching Woolley bat, again the appearance of him rather than the innings itself: so tall, and with that queer angular grace. I am tempted to remember that I can still see some of his strokes, but I expect the memory was superimposed by watching him in later years, and even more by reading Cardus. Bowes and Verity I do remember clearly from those days, and took great satisfaction as year by year they bowled out the Essex batsmen. And I have a peculiarly vivid memory of an off-drive by the Nawab of Pataudi. Worcestershire and Essex always played one another on the bank holidays, and Pataudi was playing for Worcestershire. Almost as soon as he came in, he drove Farnes, or it might have been Nichols, between cover and extra. Four runs, thank you, and the field scarcely moving. Many years later, in a Test at Leeds, I saw his son play a similar stroke which brought memory sweeping back.

And, in writing of those years at Leyton, I must tell you of a genial character from Northamptonshire, who improperly signed my autograph book while fielding at deep third man, and in consequence missed the instructions of his captain (Jupp, I think) and was resonantly and publicly denounced. I would like to thank that deep third man for his kindness, but unfortunately I never discovered his name, as his signature was totally illegible.

I never saw Bradman. He did not play when the Australians came to Leyton in 1930. I saw him later on, but it would have been nice to say that I saw him then, when even the small boys were aware that he was rending the cricketing world with his wonders. I did see another man who was in a different way a genius – George Gunn. It irritates me that though I saw George Gunn bat several times, and have an old scorecard or two to prove it, I cannot remember anything about him.

Essex then were an interesting side, though not a very good one. The best batsman in the 1920s had been Russell, who had scored centuries against Australia both at home and abroad. I only saw him play a few times for Essex, and do not remember much of him. After he retired, the small boys' hero was Jack O'Connor. O'Connor had played in a Test Match at home against South Africa in 1929, and three on tour to the West Indies the following winter. That proved to be all his Test cricket, and how we groused about it! But looking back, I suppose we did not have much of a case, because there were so many other good ones about. Robertson-Glasgow wrote of O'Connor that 'Hendren stood continually in his path to the England side'. This was not the whole truth: so did

Hammond, Leyland, Jardine, Paynter and one or two more. Still, O'Connor was unlucky not to have had a single Test against Australia (in those days, you realise, we did not think of anything as a real Test except a match against Australia: it was only in 1935, when the South Africans won a rubber over here, that we began to count the rest. I speak not only of the small boys, but most of the English cricketing public).

O'Connor was a man I remember because of the jolly ring of his name, and also because I saw him often enough to form some impression of his style. With a name like that he should have been a dasher, and so sometimes he was; but usually for Essex in the early 1930s he had to be something of a stodger, for he had not much support. He was a short but nimble man, who liked to go down the pitch to the spinners: not, it occurs to me now, unlike Hendren – which must have prompted Robertson-Glasgow to make the comparison. He bowled assorted spinners himself, and we were always crying 'Put Jack on!' when Essex needed a wicket. His hair was curly and his smile was broad. In his career, which began in 1921 and ended in 1939, he scored nearly 30,000 runs and took over 550 wickets. Do not think that I am going to give you such boring details about every cricketer I mention: but I do think that O'Connor was an underestimated player, and if you put that view down to early uncultivated enthusiasms, pray do. They say he did not much like the fast bowlers, and that he was a little slow in the field, but these refinements were beyond me then. I met him – well, not to say *met* him, but listened to him talking, and drank in his company – years later, at wartime matches and when he was a coach, first at Eton and then at Chigwell not far from Leyton. Despite his Irish name and a touch of the Irish in his character, he was very much an Essex man. His uncle, Herbert Carpenter, had played for the county for many years, and his great uncle, Robert Carpenter, would have done in the 1860s, had the Essex County Club had more than a shadowy existence then. He died aged 79 in 1977 at Buckhurst Hill also only a few miles from the Leyton ground where he scored so many runs.

Morris Nichols was the professional fast bowler (he had help from Farnes and H. D. Read) and also the number five batsman. He had not quite the glamour of O'Connor. Cardus described his gait as that of a sailor striving to keep his feet on a rolling deck. He performed his batting from a set stance with a succession of furious lunges and stabs, though it was very successful from time to time. He was chosen against Australia in 1930, did not do badly, but never played against them again. He almost certainly would have done for he was among those asked to be present at Old Trafford in 1938, but the match was a complete wash-out, the teams not finally selected since the captains did not bother to toss. This match also robbed Frank Smailes of the only chance he had of playing against Australia. However, I saw Nichols play against the West Indies in 1939. He had fourteen Tests spread over ten years, and had produced respectable figures by the end of them, his batting average slightly higher than his bowling. His fair hair seen at a distance, plastered down as was then the fashion, gave the impression of a shiny dome, and I remember we used to greet him when he came in to bat or went on to bowl, with cries of 'Come on, Baldy' – a slander, but he did not seem to mind.

The Essex opening pair, always assuming L. G. Crawley was not available (and I will come to him shortly) were Cutmore and Pope. Cutmore had been at Cambridge, without getting a Blue, and when he became a professional it was still thought a slightly unfortunate thing for a gentleman to have done. He tended to be a bit of a dasher as a batsman, and was a smart slip fielder. He usually got his thousand runs. Dudley Pope was a more solid character. He was born in Surrey, qualified for Gloucestershire but could not hold his place there, and first played for Essex in 1930. He did pretty well for them in his quiet way. He died early, and despite his seasons of service is no longer included in the *Births and Deaths* in *Wisden*. I once saw him put on 211 for the second wicket with O'Connor against Warwickshire at Leyton. The reason I remember this was that I was watching from our balcony, and mother, who had been out shopping, returned and called up to me from the ground two floors below, 'How are they doing, then?' And I replied triumphantly, 'Pope and O'Connor still in!' with such excitement that I nearly fell over the balcony. I think I was prohibited from watching from the balcony for some time thereafter. Then there was the wicket-keeper, Sheffield, who apart from being a good wicket-keeper could bat a bit. His batting average was never very high, but about twice a season he would make a fast fifty or so, usually when Essex were in a hole. Sheffield spent his winters (no doubt the stories were exaggerated by the small boys) daring the rapids of the Amazon in a small canoe.

L. G. Crawley could play only intermittently, but when he was available was sure of a place. In form, he had a mastery which no other Essex batsman of the time, not even O'Connor, possessed. When it became clear to me that I was never going to bowl like Verity, I hoped that God might permit me to bat like Crawley. The road in which we lived was Crawley Road, which I naturally assumed to have been named after him. I knew him a little many years later, when he did some reporting on cricket, though his principal game had turned out to be golf. He was one of the leading amateur golf players of his time, a member of the side which won the Walker Cup in 1938. He was golf correspondent of the *Daily Telegraph* for many years. E. W. Swanton writes of him as his 'idiosyncratic, dyspeptic, endearing' colleague. I doubt if the dyspepsia had come on when I saw him bat, but I could sense – had I known the word – that he was idiosyncratic. Sir Home Gordon, a passionate Sussex supporter, writes of a match at Leyton, when Sussex were playing there: 'Harold Gilligan and I were most anxious that his brother Arthur should declare. I even went so far as to write an estimate of what each opponent was likely to make on fourth hands, but put an X opposite Crawley.'

X was right. Crawley scored 170 and Essex won. X was always the only right thing to predict about Crawley. He told Sir Home, a long time afterwards, that he should have been out leg-before on that occasion to his first ball, but that Tate (not usually backward in such matters) had not appealed. I wish I had seen this innings.

The middle of the Essex batting was uncertain, since they had lost not only Russell, but J. W. H. T. Douglas, their captain, and a former captain of England. I have written about Douglas elsewhere, and in any case he does not really come into this book because I never saw him play. Yet I have one vivid recollection of him. He died in December 1930. He had been drowned at sea after a collision of ships in the Kattegat. It seems probable that he would have survived, had he not gone below decks in an attempt to rescue his father, who also died. When the news came, they ran up the county flag at Leyton. I asked my mother why they were flying the cricket flag in the middle of the winter, and why it was only halfway up the pole. To this day, I never see a flag at halfmast without thinking of John Douglas.

Charles Bray, whom later I came to know convivially in the press box (his essay on Douglas in *Cricket Heroes*, published by Phoenix House in 1959, is one of the best of its kind I have read) gave valuable assistance in the middle order when he had time to play, and occasionally captained the side. He was indeed captain against Yorkshire at Leyton in 1932, when Holmes and Sutcliffe scored 555 for Yorkshire's first wicket. This was then the record for any wicket anywhere, and remains the record for an opening partnership and for any wicket in England. I have written a good deal over the years about this partnership, but it has to come in again here, because it was my first great cricketing experience.

You must remember that I was conscious of being a Yorkshire boy in a strange land. When I first went to Farmer Road School (one of the big redbrick three-storeyed schools, just at the end of the road – Sherlock Holmes described them to Watson as 'lighthouses', and so, for many, they were) my Cockney classmates could not understand a word I said. One of them went home to his mother at lunchtime and said 'We got a Frenchman in our class.' I soon began to develop a line in Cockney myself and, as I have explained, became an avid supporter of Essex though when the Yorkshire team came I remembered my origins and flattened my vowels. On the Wednesday morning, 15 June 1932, I raced home and called up to father, who was, as I had expected, watching from the balcony, to demand the score. 'Yorkshire, eight for no wicket', he said. Well, that was good so far as it went.

I saw a good deal of this famous partnership. Every moment when I was not at school and play was on, I was on that balcony. I refused to go downstairs to eat. Mother was inclined to make trouble about this, but I had the support of father, who was an enthusiast himself, and promised to 'keep an eye on me' – so long as he had his meals up there too. Think what it meant to me, the little Yorkshire exile, when my very own heroes came and did this to the Londoners! Who were the Frenchmen now? At the end of the first day – I do not have to look this up – Yorkshire had scored 423 for no wicket. I remember the swift, silent running between the wickets (very different from modern Yorkshire practice) and the huge pull for six to mid-wicket with which Sutcliffe reached his 150. Next morning I raced back from school again. No wicket had fallen. It was about one o'clock that the 555 was reached (the previous record had been 554, made by two other Yorkshiremen, Brown and Tunnicliffe, in 1898). The cheering was rapturous, none more than mine. There was a big crowd by now, many Yorkshiremen having travelled south during the night. I saw Holmes and Sutcliffe stride down the pitch towards each other, majestically, and shake hands. Life, I felt, had not anything to show more fair, though I did not put it that way; and I am not sure that it has had.

However, I soon learnt that bliss does not long remain un-alloyed. Next ball, Sutcliffe, taking a wild swish at Eastman, was bowled. By this time I was in the ground itself, nobody bothering to keep children out in all the excitement. Holmes (224 not out) and Sutcliffe (313) were assembled to be photographed under the scoreboard. Suddenly the total on the board moved back to 554. There had been disagreement between the scorers about a no-ball. Had they only equalled the record, not broken it? There was a time of agonised suspense, and then the board moved back to 555. There has been much research into which was the true figure, none of it, I think, conclusive. I would not be surprised if both were wrong; we shall never know. Before modern scoring techniques were invented, in the first place by Arthur Wrigley, and then developed by Roy Webber, Bill Frindall, Irving Rosenwater and several more – scoring in first-class cricket was haphazard. It was commonplace for one scorer to 'take a stroll round the ground' for half an hour, and then fill in his book from his colleague's, while the colleague in turn took his stroll. Something like this, I expect, had happened at Leyton. I like the story that it was a little parson (Essex grounds have always seemed to harbour a lot of parsons) arriving with his own scorebook, meticulously kept, who settled the argument.

I am sure that many of the famous close finishes of the past, say Australia's win by three runs at Old Trafford in 1902, or Gloucestershire's by a run against Yorkshire in 1906 (the year when Yorkshire were said to have lost the championship by 'one run') were decided by casual scoring, as much as anything that actually happened on the field of play. This point is brought out by John Marchant in *The Greatest Test Match*, published by Faber and Gwyer in 1926. It is an account of the last Test at the Oval that year, when England recovered the Ashes. Mr Marchant consulted the scorebook, and found that in a number of instances it made no sense at all. The book the England scorer had used was an old Surrey second eleven book of twenty years before. When some-one wanted to make a detailed reconstruction of Bradman's 334 at Leeds in 1930, the then record Test score, Arthur Wrigley was asked to help, and consulted the scorebook. He found it was impossible to give a ball-by-ball statistical account of the innings. It was this which led him to work out his own method of scoring, with its inbuilt checks. But it was a long time before any of the county scorers adopted it.

The muddle and delay over the Holmes-Sutcliffe record slightly flawed my delight. My Cockney friends were not slow to suggest that they had only broken it by 'cheating'. And it was the second such irritation in a few months, because I had supported New-castle United against Arsenal in the FA Cup final, and though Newcastle duly won, it was only through a disputed goal, which no Londoner, certainly no other Farmer Road boy, would admit was valid. But I must return to that incident later, when I come to a consideration of the power of prayer in sport.

When Essex decided to leave Leyton in 1934, I thought they had done me a dirty trick, and for a long time my attitude towards them was malevolent. I rejoiced when they lost and mourned when they won: never more so than when they got Yorkshire out for thirty-one and ninety-nine at Huddersfield in 1935, winning by an innings and hundreds. We were on holiday in Cornwall at the time, but did not altogether escape the humiliation: several members of my father's congregation and their children sent us revengeful postcards. I was still able to see Essex from time to time at places such as Ilford and Brentwood – always cheering for their opponents – and as I grew older I was allowed to make trips to Lord's and the Oval. But it was difficult and expensive, in comparison with the delights that had been constantly on my doorstep. That cricketless Leyton ground mocked me. Nothing seemed to happen there, except large policemen running races very slowly. (It was the Metropolitan Police who had bought the ground.)

It was only many years later, when I had met Trevor Bailey and Douglas Insole, that I really became reconciled to Essex cricket. I have been back to Leyton once or twice since they started playing there again. Bernard Darwin said that it is usually a mistake to revisit the scenes of childhood delights: they were better kept fresh in the memory, untarnished by reality. But I have enjoyed going back there. How much smaller the ground seemed! E. W. Swanton called it 'that grimy yet not wholly unattractive enclosure which had brought all the great cricketers, in their time, to the East Londoner's doorstep'. It is not so grimy now, either. If it was Yorkshire that gave me a taste for cricket, it was Leyton that gratified it. Had my father been called to, say, Stepney or

Walthamstow, I might never have been seized by cricket at all. As it was, the game became a passion, and remained one for many years.

II

A Cricketer at the Breakfast Table

For the elemental creatures go
About my table to and fro
Yeats

When it rained at Leyton, I would go indoors and play cricket at home. I played it by myself, for I was an only child, save a little sister who had died too young even to field. It would be wrong to say that the death of Marjorie meant a lot to me at the time, for I was still only six myself. The shock passed and childish resilience reasserted itself. Many years later, on a train going to one of the Essex grounds, I passed the vast dreary municipal cemetery where she was buried. By then I had a small daughter of my own, and felt a rush of emotion. I would have liked to get out and seek her grave, but the train went steadily on to Chelmsford, or wherever it was. I wrote a little about her in my report for *The Times* that evening, but they cut it out.

Playing cricket by yourself is not much fun. Besides, it kicked up too much of a din in the hall. I soon devised a better system, with the assistance of my lead soldiers, of which I had a large and varied collection. I played with them on the bedroom floor, using one hand for batting and the other for bowling. I soon learnt to keep a rough score, and father, seeing that I was working at it, bought me a scorebook. I must have filled dozens of those shilling scorebooks. When Essex were doing badly, I would replay the match in the bedroom, pausing only to shout downstairs to mother 'O'Connor's got his hundred', or similar glad tidings. I wish I had kept some of those scorebooks, but all those records of mighty Essex victories in the early 1930s are lost. Nor did I confine myself to county cricket. I was an assiduous reader of the *Gem* and *Magnet*, and created matches between St Jim's and Greyfriars, the two schools (I suppose I must explain to the modern generation) that featured in those publications. I was always inclined to be a St Jim's man myself, but Greyfriars took some beating, and one of the most famous pairs ever to open an innings on that bedroom floor were Harry Wharton and Bob Cherry. Farmer Road School also played matches there, and I stooped to include myself in the eleven. I did not overdo things by scoring centuries. It was my habit to bat at, say, number seven, and make a careful, match winning twenty-five or so. It was a nice blue carpet with a good pile. The gas fire was at one end, the cabin trunk at the other, and this was how I always thought of the ends, whoever was playing. Some of the fieldsmen necessarily had to be placed under the bed, which involved much bending and stretching on my part at the end of each over. I can remember now the sense of it, the smell of it. One small boy crawling around with his soldiers on the floor: and all the magic of Lord's and Greyfriars. I can see Larwood as he came on from the cabin trunk end – Essex fifteen to win and a couple of wickets left – in all the majesty of a Zulu warrior.

For though I have called these toys my 'soldiers', they were an assortment, by no means all military. There were cowboys, Indians, and even civilians, relics of a Hornby railway. One of these, a plump middle-aged gentleman with a bowler hat, represented Hobbs, when he happened to be playing, and I think never anyone else. That was how we thought of Hobbs then: senior, apart, not to be impersonated. You knew he would be travelling first class. The Zulu warrior was always the fast bowler. If he was not being Larwood, he was Nichols or Farnes or Hurree Jamset Ram Singh. My supply of 'soldiers' was not sufficient to allow every cricketer to have only one incarnation. When I played myself, I went to the wicket as a sailor. There gradually developed a division between the soldiers (red coats) and the others. My side was 'the others', so they usually won. But the soldiers possessed a marvellous slow left-arm bowler. He had originally been the player of the big drum in the Coldstream Guards band (a splendid Christmas present from one of the wealthier members of father's congregation). He had lost his drum and his head, and there was a hole in his chest where the drum had been attached, but I had a great affection for him. In the winter, when I turned my attention to football, he played inside-left much in the manner of Alex James, lying cunningly behind the rest of the forwards, the midfield link.

I do not think I ever really lost the delight of my lead soldiers' cricket. It was just that as I grew older I became rather ashamed of playing with them and would wait till my parents were out: once they came back early, and found me on the blue carpet with the whole gallery set out, and I felt a bit silly, especially as I was giving a running commentary ('Now it's Hurree Singh again to Tom Merry . . .'). So I progressed from carpet cricket to table cricket. There have been many varieties of this. In one form or another, it is probably as old as the game itself. There is a pleasant account of one variation in Eric Parker's book, *Playing Fields*, published in 1922. The book was in some ways Eton's answer to *Tom Brown's Schooldays*. I found it rather dull, and have never been tempted to read it again, but I must say in its defence that Bernard Darwin liked it. On a rainy day, two young Etonians were playing table cricket.

> You wrote down the names of two elevens on two sheets of paper and then dotted a pencil with your eyes shut on another piece of paper, which was marked with 'fourers', 'sixers', 'caught', 'bowled' and so on.
> 'That's another six to W.G. By Jove, he is hitting. That's seven out of the ground now. That makes him 202.'
> 'Bet he'll soon be bowled, then.'
> 'Bet he isn't.'
> 'There you are, then. Bowled Spofforth. Told you so.'
> 'Well, he's made two hundred, anyhow. Spofforth's average must be simply rotten.'
> 'Ass! He's only just gone on.'
> 'Why didn't you put him on before, then? Just shows.'

But this was a primitive form of the table game, though widely played. If you had enough patience, you could allow nearly every possibility to be taken into account. Robertson-Glasgow once found a couple of youngsters who had a square marked 'PM', which stood for 'pulled muscle'. It is, however, too chancy to give a realistic representation of cricket on a scoresheet, and the temptations to dishonesty, by the merest winking of an eye as you stab at the sheet, are more than most schoolboys can withstand. A better variation is to choose a page of a book opened at random and take the letters on the page one by one, each representing a ball and its outcome. This rules out cheating but limits variety since there are only twenty-six letters in the alphabet. It was in this form of the game that Robertson-Glasgow himself, who had chosen a team of composers against a team of authors, suddenly found that one of his principal batsmen, Beethoven, had been run out. He at once envisaged the scene: 'Ah, deaf, poor chap. Never heard the call.'

Another way of playing indoors is to write out the various possibilities on triangular sections of a circular cardboard disc. You then, with a compass, impale the disc at the centre and spin it. The other half of the compass holds a pencil and, when the spinning disc has come to rest, the pencil tells you what has happened according to which section it is pointing. I had a lot of fun with devices of this kind, several of which were marketed, though I am sure it was the small boys who first had the idea. With a little ingenuity it was possible to produce a convincing looking scoresheet. The crucial point is that you need to have more than one disc: three is really the minimum. The first applies to numbers one to four in the order, the second to numbers five to eight, the third to numbers nine to eleven. The chances are apportioned so that the earlier batsmen are likely to score more runs than the later, while your number one could still score nought and your number eleven a century (because, if one of your first four stayed in, his partners could continue to bat on the same disc).

There were games played with packs of cards. And I remember affectionately a handy pocket game called 'Owzthat?', which you could carry with you on trains and trams, and even play in class, if you did not get too excited and sat at the back of the room. I saw it, or something very like it, in a shop only a year or two ago. There were two small hexagonal cylinders, which would go into a tin smaller than a matchbox. The sides of the first were marked 6–4–3–2–1–Owzthat? You rolled it, and if Owzthat? turned up you rolled the second, which was inscribed 'Bowled-caught-stumped-lbw-run out-not out'. Many of my childhood sicknesses were made more pleasant by 'Owzthat?'. You could play it in bed on a tray, or even a plate, so long as you had a pencil and a pad to keep the score.

All of these – and there must have been many more which I never encountered or have forgotten – performed their service without being altogether satisfactory. Then, round about 1937, there came on the market a game called *Stumpz*. *Stumpz* revolutionised table cricket. It was played with a board, marked into sections, representing a cricket field. There were eleven counters to be used as fieldsmen, and disposed on the appropriate sections. The batsman and bowler each held a pack of cards. There was an indicator, which could be adjusted to show whether the ball was straight, a leg-break, an off-break, or a googly. The bowler could choose to place his card in one of three spaces: to the off, to the leg, or on the wicket. That expressed his intentions. Then he turned his card up and it showed what length the ball turned out to be: a good length, a half volley, a long hop, and so on. This frequently showed, as all bowlers have discovered, that subtle intentions are not always equalled by skill of execution. The batsman then declared the stroke with which he would meet it, before turning up *his* card. He could play forward or back, he could cut, on-drive, off-drive, leg glance – there was a choice of about ten strokes. The batsman's card showed what had happened. This was the basis of the game, though there were certain refinements, including wides, no-balls, yorkers and dropped catches. A good deal of care had obviously gone into the preparation of the cards, and if you played the correct stroke you were likelier to make runs than if you did not.

But there were snags for the addict even with *Stumpz*. Since it was a parlour game and parlours had other uses, it had to be planned to finish in a reasonable time, a few hours at most. In consequence the cards could not be contrived to give an accurate replica of a first-class match, or even a club match, since an over could easily take as long as it would have done on a field of play. So the inventors had, understandably, speeded it up. However skilfully you batted, the average score for a team's innings was little more than a hundred. Something had to happen every ball. Less than once an over would the combination of cards produce the result, 'No score'. I wanted a closer approximation to the real thing. Consider such a bowling analysis as this, and England against Australia too:

	O.	M.	R.	W.
Farnes	5.4	0	54	4
Bowes	5	0	46	6

Absurd: but *Stumpz* seemed to have the right idea, and I set myself (I was about fifteen then) to improve it.

The first step was to compile my own sets of cards for the bowlers and batsmen, and it took much trial and error to get the balance right. I increased the number of strokes available, and the range of balls that could be bowled (particularly, I included a large number of bowlers' cards marked 'Just short of a length' – a result of observation). The main thing was to slow down the rate of scoring to something nearer a normal pace. Of course, this meant that a three-day match would take around three days to play: but I was only playing by myself, and holidays were long.

I kept at this for years, constantly introducing new subtleties, and in the end managed to produce a game which, I think, set down ball by ball in a scorebook, could not be distinguished from a real one. It was, naturally, completely unmarketable, but it comforted me especially during the early years of the war, when so little cricket was going on. Some snags I never overcame. Time was one. In the end I settled for three minutes to the over, assuming that the fast bowlers and the slow ones would cancel each other out. It would be a large assumption today, but at that time twenty overs to the hour was considered an acceptable minimum. Interruptions from the weather solved themselves. In a small house it was not often possible to keep my apparatus, which covered a medium-sized table, intact between sessions. Mother would descend and remove it, and cards would have to be reshuffled later, and a new start made from the moment of interruption. Mother represented the weather. I developed a complicated system, depending chiefly on the throwing of dice, to decide whether she had inflicted a light shower, nothing more than a ten-minute break, or anything above it right up to the disaster of 'match abandoned'. She was a forbearing mother, and on the whole my table summers were bedevilled less by rain than a normal English one.

I was able to deal with the use of the new ball by bringing into force some supplementary cards for an arbitrary period (usually about ten overs). You could never take into account variations in the pitch. In Stumpz cricket, even in my sophisticated version, we had covered wickets all the time, long before the practice was adopted so unfortunately in the first-class game. Another difficulty was left-handers: to have reproduced them on the board meant not just a doubling but a quadrupling of all packs of cards, and I already had about six. In the end, after long procrastination I tackled the job, and weeks of labour produced the sets of cards.

But I had left it too late. I was growing older. Girls, and Mozart, and Oliver Cromwell, were rivalling Bradman and Hutton in my thoughts. The final, perfected edition of my game was scarcely ever played. It thus confirmed one of the theories of Professor Parkinson, who pointed out that the League of Nations building at Geneva was only completed in 1940.

All the same, I look back upon the achievement with some small pride, and it was a more enjoyable form of vicarious cricket than I could have found in computer games. You can cheat a bit when you are playing against yourself. I tried hard not to do so consciously, but it was undeniable that Yorkshire beat Lancashire more often than they lost, and the same applied to England against Australia. And on one occasion, when I organised a knock-out competition involving both major and minor counties (here again I was ahead of my time) Cornwall, where I was then living, had a suspiciously long run.

It occurs to me that the advent of one-day cricket, especially the forty-over Sunday League, offers the chance of a game of table cricket which would not take too long to play, but would still bear a resemblance to the quasi first-class game as we now see it. Thus the gap between the facts of the field and the necessities of the parlour could be bridged. I would not any longer be tempted to play it myself.

I doubt if I have succeeded in communicating adequately my feelings about these experiences, which were so private that nobody else could fully share in them, or understand them. The emotion I felt when Hobbs was batting, black city coat and walking stick, was entirely my own. However, boys, sometimes even adults, will continue to enjoy cricket in these varieties. My own children have done so. The only difference is that 'Another six for W.G.' becomes 'Another six for Gower'. And apart from enjoying it, I did derive an unexpected benefit from it. For when as time passed, I was asked to give cricket commentaries for the BBC, I did not feel I was facing something entirely new. Crouched over my soldiers and my packs of cards, I had been doing it for years.

III

Cider Country

In 1936, I was sent to school at Taunton, and this brought Somerset into my picture of cricket. It is odd that I cannot remember Somerset playing at Leyton. I should certainly have seen them in 1932, when, a fortnight after the Holmes/Sutcliffe match, Essex took another hiding. Somerset scored 455 in the first innings, John and Frank Lee putting on 234 for the first wicket, and won by an innings, despite brave efforts by Crawley and Pope. But I have looked this up in *Wisden*: I do not remember it. I think we must have been away on holiday in Ilkley. I know it was about Wimbledon time, because that year Bunny Austin reached the final, and I had to invent a form of tennis with ping-pong bats – left hand against right – to demonstrate that Austin had *really* beaten Vines. And I know that I did this in a garden at Ilkley, up Cowpasture Road, not far from the moor. It was the garden of Miss Whitwam, who ran a guest house there. Miss Whitwam had been my first Primary Sunday School leader, a nice woman, who no doubt gave the family favourable terms for this return trip. *And* I can tell you that we were shown the visitors' book, which contained the signature of Henry Ainley. He had gone there shortly before for a rest cure (I suspect, looking back, because it was a long way from the nearest pub). The name meant nothing to me at the time, but afterwards whenever we heard him on the radio, mother would remind me that we had stayed at the same guest house as Henry Ainley, and I would swell my breast with pride. The left hand against right hand ping-pong in the garden had a small consequence, too, because when I came to take up tennis myself (and I was not all that bad, house colours at school) I discovered that I was ambidextrous at tennis, an uncommon thing then.

But I have digressed from Somerset. They were a side with much appeal. Everyone except their immediate opponents, and Gloucestershire, liked to see them win. This remained true until the last few years, when they have started winning competitions, though still not, as I write in 1984, the championship. In those days one was always faintly surprised to discover them in the top half of the championship table, and over the years they have lost more matches than they have won. But they had a knack of achieving victories against strong sides, from improbable positions. The most famous example of this was against Yorkshire in 1901, at Leeds. Somerset won the toss, batted, and were bowled out by Rhodes, Hirst and Haigh for eighty-seven. Yorkshire made a poor start but led on the first innings by 238. On the second day Somerset went in again. L. C. H. Palairet scored 173, Braund, who opened with him, 107, F. A. Phillips (who was scarcely heard of before or after – he was an amateur who could not play often) 122. There were some dropped chances, and an umpire's decision over which Yorkshiremen grieved for years. The final score was 630. In the last innings Yorkshire were bowled out for 113, demoralised, while Somerset were laughing their heads off. The next season at Sheffield, Somerset beat them again, though this was not so dramatic. It was a low scoring match, much interrupted by weather, won by thirty-four runs. Braund, who bowled leg-spin even more effectively than he batted (he was in the strong England side of that year) had most to do with it. These were the only two matches Yorkshire lost in the three seasons 1900 to 1902, when they won three championships in a row. And in 1903, with a slice or two of luck, Somerset beat them again at Taunton.

I had not been at Taunton School for long before I heard vaguely of these famous victories, especially when I revealed my Yorkshire sympathies. For some reason Yorkshire did not play Somerset in the championship at that time, and it was the unanimous view among the Somerset supporters (there were a lot of them, because there were nearly as many day boys in the school as boarders) that Yorkshire funked them. Bridling as I did at this slur, I became very fond of Somerset cricket. They established themselves firmly in second place in my affections, replacing the truant Essex.

And indeed, Somerset in those last few years before the war were something of a boy's dream. They had only six full-time professionals – seven when Buse joined in 1938 – and the amateurs who filled up the side were full of talent, gaiety and eccentricity. Nor were the professionals from a common mould. There was Gimblett to open the innings, and Wellard to bat in the late middle order. No other batsmen of the time caused such a wriggling of boyish expectation when they came in – well, there was a splendid man called Watt, of Kent, but he did not come off very often. There was also, I realise now, Jim Smith of Middlesex, but I never had the luck to see him score any runs to speak of. Somerset also had Bill Andrews to use the new ball with Wellard, Hazell to bowl slow left arm, Luckes to keep wicket. And they had Frank Lee, who scored many runs for them, but of whom my memories are less entertaining, though I found him a very pleasant fellow in later years when he was umpiring. I was unlucky with the tribe of Lee. The first time I ever went to Lord's, H. W. Lee batted interminably for not very many, on a damp and chilly day. I recall another prolonged but unexciting effort by G. M. Lee of Derbyshire, I think at Leyton but it may have been on another of the Essex grounds. As for Frank, it seemed to me in those days that I always got to the Taunton ground (these visits were haphazard, because of school disciplines) just as Gimblett was out, and Lee nicely settled in. He would then bat urbanely for the hour or two which was all for which I could stay, and get out just as I was departing for call-over, and some such hitter as E. F. Longrigg or H. D. Burrough coming out of the pavilion.

There was a magnificent game at Taunton, at Whitsuntide in 1938, when Gloucestershire came to play – it is still the 'bank holiday' match between the two counties, though they have changed the dates of the bank holidays. I cannot now remember just how much of this match I managed to see. I know that for part of the Monday, holiday though it was, I was engaged at school, playing for the fourth eleven. At Taunton School, Whitsun was the occasion for the Old Boys' reunion, and these celebrations were not always entirely a delight to those still in residence (those who did not live near enough to get home for the weekend). On this occasion, bursting with zeal to renew the athletic exploits of the past, the Old Boys had produced six or seven sides to play the school at cricket. A good deal of impressment went on regarding the smaller boys before the numbers could be made up. We were keen enough on cricket, but for the lesser elevens the proposition was hopeless, and we would rather have watched the first eleven match, or slip down to the county ground to watch Wellard bowling to Hammond. I had mixed feelings about being chosen for the fourth eleven. I opened the innings, and was given out leg-before-wicket to the first ball. It was an appalling decision, given by a nervous schoolboy umpire at the behest of a very large, red-faced and loud-voiced Old Boy, who had not taken a wicket in many years. We were all out for 25 or so, and by lunch the Old Boys were something like 140 for 3. It was very hot. The day stretched aridly ahead, for clearly every Old Boy was intent on having a knock, and telling the members of his club about it later ('Can still play a bit, you know; got a quick fifty down at the old school last week'). However, their enthusiasm was diminished by a lunchtime visit to the Staplegrove Inn, and soon afterwards they called it a day, having successfully combated the aridity.

I reached the county ground in time to see the end of the Somerset innings. The score was rather disappointing, because although they led by fifty-odd, they had looked as if they would lead by many more. That evening and the following morning, Hammond batted. Then there was a Gloucestershire declaration, and Somerset had to score nearly 300 to win with no time to waste. Somerset won by a wicket, Luckes hitting two boundaries in what would in any case have been the last over. The second and winning boundary was a difficult chance to Jack Crapp in the outfield. He did right to dive forward for it, but could not quite get his grasp upon it.

I saw cricket on all three days of this match, but no, I cannot really remember how much. Certainly, however, this was my first revelation of Hammond, and I was now old enough to notice something of how he made his strokes. The famous off-drive was working well. He cut a lot. Also, I testify, in this innings he used the pull, a stroke which it is always said he had abandoned years earlier: it was not quite a hook; but he was aiming towards mid-wicket off the front foot. I can see one now which he did not quite middle, but which went safely between mid-wicket and long-leg, first bounce into the Somerset Stragglers' pavilion. I know I missed the finish, but the day boys recounted the story to us next day, in graphic and widely varying accounts. Years later Jack Crapp told me about it too. And there is a splendid account of it in *Sixty Years of Somerset Cricket* (Westaway Books, 1952) by R. A.

Roberts. Ron Roberts's early death was a heavy loss to Somerset cricket. In his relatively short life, he had established himself as one of the most reliable and influential writers on the game. He was a member of the Somerset committee, and had he lived would have surely saved the county from many of the administrative muddles and quarrels which beset it in the following years.

I am not going to cumber this book with many scorecards, but this is one, not often reproduced, which deserves remembrance:

GLOUCESTERSHIRE

Mr B. O. Allen, c Lyon, b Hazell	52	run out		28
C. J. Barnett, lbw b Wellard	41	c and b Wellard		0
G. M. Emmett, b Wellard	18	lbw b Wellard		6
Mr W. R. Hammond, c Luckes, b Hazell	6	not out		140
J. F. Crapp, b Buse	33	b Wellard		29
W. L. Neale, c Luckes, b Hazell	13	c Luckes, b Wellard		6
Mr B. H. Lyon, c Gimblett, b Hazell	0	c Longrigg, b Hazell		88
R. A. Sinfield, b Wellard	0	not out		0
E. A. Wilson, b Andrews	38	c Andrews, b Kinnersley		32
C. J. Scott, lbw b Andrews	9			
M. Cranfield, not out	5			
Extras: 1b, 3lb, 1w, 1nb	6	4b, 3lb, 2nb		9
	221	For 7 wickets, declared		**338**

	O.	M.	R.	W.	O.	M.	R.	W.
Wellard	30	6	77	3	32	7	85	4
Andrews	15.1	0	48	2	13	1	76	0
Buse	17	4	48	1	27	6	86	0
Hazell	16	2	42	4	27	6	72	1
Kinnersley					5	2	10	1

SOMERSET

H. Gimblett, c Wilson, b Emmett	67	c Allen, b Sinfield		7
F. S. Lee, lbw b Sinfield	56	c Allen, b Barnett		18
Mr M. D. Lyon, b Hammond	48	lbw b Barnett		19
H. T. F. Buse, c Wilson, b Scott	27	c Emmett, b Hammond		79
Mr E. F. Longrigg, c Hammond, b Sinfield	7	b Sinfield		24
Mr J. W. Seamer, c Allen, b Scott	23	run out		34
W. H. R. Andrews, c Wilson b Barnett	6	c Barnett, b Emmett		2
Mr K. C. Kinnersley, c Allen, b Scott	12	c and b Emmett		7
A. W. Wellard, b Hammond	21	c Barnett, b Scott		68
W. T. Luckes, lbw b Scott	2	not out		18
H. L. Hazell, not out	0	not out		0
Extras: 1b, 4lb, 1w, 1nb	7	7b, 1lb		8
	276	For 9 wickets		**284**

	O.	M.	R.	W.	O.	M.	R.	W.
Hammond	33.2	8	64	2	17	3	57	1
Scott	19	2	42	4	15	3	51	1
Sinfield	39	20	57	2	29.4	10	68	2
Barnett	10	1	20	1	17	5	50	2
Cranfield	6	0	33	0	2	0	5	0
Emmett	9	1	52	1	6	0	36	2
Neale					2	0	9	0

Somerset won by one wicket.

There were seven past or future Test players in this match (remember Tests were much more of a rarity then). Hammond was England's captain against Australia that year. Barnett was chosen for four Tests (he only played in three, because of the Old Trafford wash-out), Sinfield and Wellard in one each. Gimblett had played for England for the first time in the previous year; Emmett and Crapp did so after the war. You will notice, however, the absence of one famous name. Tom Goddard was injured, and I suppose he might well have made a difference in the last hectic phase, when Wellard was hitting six sixes and five fours.

I must dwell a little on some of the Somerset cricketers of those days, though I must not dwell upon them too long, or I shall need another book. But I must say something of Wellard, the most regular hitter of sixes the game has ever known. Ron Roberts says that of Wellard's 12,000 runs in first-class cricket, about a quarter were hit in sixes. One cannot place this among the Frindall tablets of stone, because until about 1910 a hit which did not bounce before the boundary usually counted only four. To score six, you had to hit the ball *outside the walls of the ground*. Thus Albert Trott's famous smack over the pavilion at Lords only counted four, because it bounced off a chimney pot and did not pass the wall behind. And Jessop, the most obvious example, must have hit goodness knows how many balls for what would now be counted six but only showed as four in the scorebooks. Still, it is fairly safe to say that there has been no better hitter of sixes than Arthur Wellard. Roberts said of him:

He was given natural resources as a fast bowler and hitter that won him a place in the hearts of cricketers everywhere . . . For bowling, a big strong frame, as tough as teak, a lion's heart, strong fingers, and a natural, easy action. For batting, strength again, but an eagle eye, too, and the gift of being able to hit great

distances with his firm-footed swing. For fielding, courage,
which enabled him to follow the ball closely off the bat's face,
even when squatting just a few yards away, and, of course,
tough, capacious hands.

He preferred to drive straight or to long-on, and also preferred
to bat at the pavilion end, because he liked to hear the splash when
the ball reached the River Tone. But I remember a time when,
batting from the river end, a vast pull landed on the bridge,
whence it bounced into the cattle market, alarming a bull and
several farmers who were negotiating about its future.

But we ought not to think of Wellard primarily as a hitter. His
principal function was to be a fast-medium bowler. He took more
than 1600 wickets. He played in two Test matches but you could
not say that in this he was unlucky, for England had many good
bowlers of about his pace in the late 1930s. He was chosen for the
second Test against New Zealand in 1937, and took four of the first
six New Zealand wickets, Vivian, Kerr, Donnelly and Hadlee,
for eighty-one. He was chosen for the Australian match at
Lord's in 1938, but did not do quite enough to hold his place.
He tried to emulate Albert Trott's famous six, but the bowler was
O'Reilly, and he was caught in the deep by McCormick. I can
remember that Howard Marshall said on the radio that he
thought it was the highest, as opposed to the longest, hit ever
made at Lord's.

In 1946, when the supply of England fast bowlers had dwindled,
he would have been a sure choice for Tests, had he been ten years
younger ... ah! had he been ten years younger. He reached his
best at the wrong time, something that is liable to happen to
cricketers, especially when there are wars about. Robertson-
Glasgow thought that Wellard's chief quality as a cricketer was
that he could 'keep it up', referring less to his length than his
perseverance. 'He could watch the ineptitude of a slip-fielder with
a smile of resignation, almost of sympathy. He was intelligent and
observant.' This is a high compliment from such a source.

Although he looked, and came to talk, every inch and vowel like
a Somerset man, Wellard was born in Kent, and would have played
for them had they taken any notice of him. But his natural home
proved to be down by Mendip and Quantock and Brendon. It is
strange how many cricketers from foreign parts have come to
settle for Somerset as their home. Wellard from Kent, Woods and

Alley from Australia, Atkinson (the present president) from Northumberland . . . it would be easy to make a long list.

Bill Andrews, who was Wellard's opening bowling partner, though not born locally, also became one of Somerset's own, and remains so. Whenever I enter a Somerset ground, I cock an ear to hear if Bill's about, and can usually detect him. He was a pretty good fast-medium right-hander, not quite in the England class, though he firmly believes that in the 1938 season "twas a toss-up between me and Arthur'. He twice did 'the double', a thousand runs and a hundred wickets. Although I did not see very much of him as a cricketer, I have seen a good deal of him off the field, when he has sometimes acted as number two in the commentary box, explosively (he stammers a bit when he grows excited) summarising the shortcomings of later generations. Bill's broadcasts were like Oliver Cromwell's speeches: the grammar uncertain, but the meaning coming forcefully through. I was in much awe of him, of course, when I first met him. At Taunton in 1948, the Australian match when I was first auditioned for commentary, Bill was present, perched on the crowded and unstable commentary scaffolding. After I had had my audition, he shook me warmly by the hand saying 'B-bloody good, b-bloody good'. The proper commentator was John Arlott – it was also the first time I had met *him*. His only comment on my performance was a long-drawn-out 'Aar'gh'. I spent the train journey back to Plymouth pondering on the *nuances* of that 'Aar'gh'. But I could always reassure myself, with more hope than conviction, with the praise of W. H. R. Andrews.

In 1973 Bill Andrews, as he had always been threatening, published a book. It was called *The Hand that Bowled Bradman*. I asked the editor of *The Cricketer* if I could review it: less, I think it is fair to say, for the prospect of the fee (in those days only very rich and very poor men wrote for *The Cricketer*) but because I wanted to give Bill a leg-up. One way and another, he had been having rather a rough time (he claims to have been sacked by Somerset five times in five different capacities). This is part of what I wrote.

Bill Andrews played for Somerset from 1930 to 1947. He bowled fast-medium, mostly inswingers, and batted lustily around number seven. He is an immensely genial, immensely kind, immensely voluble and immensely tactless man. The slight stammer from which he suffers, and of which he makes some play in the book, was surely a gift from an anxious guardian angel, a forlorn attempt to stop him from putting his foot in his mouth as soon as he opens it. There is no malice nor guile in him, though he is at times capable of a certain low cunning, of the kind which would not deceive an infant. Anyone who told me he did not *like* Bill would go down in my esteem (though anyone who told me he had never been irritated by him would go down too, for quite different reasons).

I interpose a story of Bill at the Scarborough Festival. Life and wine used to run freely at the Scarborough Festival, but one night Bill had gone rather far, and got into a heavy argument with, of all people, Sir Pelham Warner. The next morning, in the lounge before breakfast, his friends were telling him that he ought to apologise. Bill boomingly declared that he would do no such thing, but ultimately bowed to pressure, and declared, 'ALL RIGHT, then, ALL RIGHT, I'll apologise to the silly old b-b' – and then, after a startled glance at someone who had just come in and was standing at his shoulder, continued without a pause, 'Oh, good morning, Sir Pelham.' But I resume the review:

The book is readable, often funny, and gives a lively picture of a professional cricketer's life in the 'thirties and 'forties. It is good value for money, as book prices go. It does not consistently capture the authentic Andrews flavour. This is because, although he has been a reporter, the written word is not Bill's *métier*. He tells us how a friend of his, a master at Colston's School, Bristol, would write on the blackboard, every Monday morning, excerpts from the Andrews column in the *Bristol Evening Post*, and tell his class 'Now turn that into English'.

In his preface, Bill acknowledges a collaboration with David Foot, an admirable journalist. I understand that collaboration was necessary, because Bill had written about two and a half times the length required, and though the publishers asked him to shorten it, it was agony for him to take out a precious sentence, only to be eased by adding an extra one.

He takes the title of his book from a story that he has often told. He did bowl Bradman, though Bradman had scored 202 at the time, and Bill thinks that for once the little something-or-other gave it away. 'Shake the hand that bowled Bradman!' he roars to friends, and (occasionally) complete strangers, and plunges into the tale. I heard him tell it last on May 27, when he was watching the John Player League match at Bristol between Somerset and Gloucestershire. He does not think all that much of 40-over cricket. But you will all be pleased to know that he was in capital nick, wistfully hoping for yet another job for Somerset, so that he could be sacked again.

After I had written the first draft of this review, I showed it to my friend David Foot, who made one or two corrections and suggestions, but agreed that it ought to please Bill. A few weeks after the review was published, I was in the commentary box at the Weston Festival, and saw Bill striding purposefully towards it. Eager for his meed of praise, I hopped out of the box, my hand outstretched. He shook it solemnly.

The normal salutations done, I said bashfully, 'Did you – er did you see the little piece I wrote in *The Cricketer?*'

He gazed at me. After a pause he said: 'Some liked it. I'm told some liked it. I thought it was b-bloody awful.' He paused again, as if to reconsider. I sensed he was thinking deeply about his choice of a word. 'No', he said, 'we've been friends a long time. 'Twasn't bloody awful. But mind, 'twas bloody terrible'.

The third Somerset cricketer of those prewar years whom I remember vividly was Harold Gimblett. Many years afterwards I was honoured to be asked to speak at his memorial service, at St James's Church by the ground. John Arlott read the lesson, and the Bishop of Taunton gave the blessing. It was a moving occasion, when the pride of Somerset saluted one of their own. Harold was a little like Hamlet playing – no, not the clown, but perhaps Laertes. He batted then, and even in his later career after the war, like a country lad, without a care in the world (though I am not suggesting his style was bucolic). Most of those who watched him, and even met him, took him for a cheerful extrovert. This was wrong. He thought a lot, worried a lot, fretted a lot, all the more because he struggled to present a calm, bold front to the outer world. Once when I was in a mental hospital, feeling very sorry for myself, he wrote me a letter full of understanding and wise advice, and thereafter we sometimes talked of mental stresses. It did not come as a total surprise to learn that he died after taking an overdose of drugs. He had been suffering acutely from arthritis, which provided 'giant despair' with a spur.

Harold was born in 1914, in Bicknoller, a Quantock village. The story of his entry to first-class cricket has often been told, but is always worth retelling. He was a promising player from an early age, and made a reputation in village and club cricket. At the beginning of the 1935 season, he was offered a month's trial with Somerset. A fortnight passed, he had not been chosen for the county side, and had been warned that his contract was unlikely to be renewed. Then, for the match against Essex at Frome, Somerset found themselves a man short, not an improbable situation in those days. Gimblett was summoned from the family farm near Watchet, on the north coast, more than fifty miles away. He went in at number eight, when the score was 107 for 6, and made a century in 63 minutes, which, as it proved, was the fastest of the season, and won him the newly invented John Lawrence Trophy. He made 123 in all, with three sixes and seventeen fours. It is a small ground, but there were some good Essex bowlers: Nichols (who took most of the wickets), the steady Eastman and the two Smiths, Ray and Peter. Ray was considered for England sides, and Peter, after the war, did play for England, in Australia, though by then he was past his best.

Immediately after this match, Gimblett went to Lord's, and scored fifty against Middlesex. By this time he had become what Priestley in another context called a *wonder boy*. A chartered aeroplane flew to Somerset, so that he could be photographed on the family farm. The press burbled with his praise. I do not think this treatment did his cricket or character much harm, but equally it did it no good. It left him vulnerable when, inevitably, he could not live up to that remarkable start. His average at the end of the season was under twenty. It was a useful beginning really, but so much had been expected of him that he expected too much of himself.

When I went to Taunton School, the day boys were full of Gimblett, though it was sometimes said that he was conceited (the modern word would be 'big-headed'). This was unjustified, but small boys being what they are – they expected him to score a hundred every time – understandable. They had to make excuses when the sixes had not gone over the boundary, but skied into the hands of midwicket. 'My Dad says he's getting too big for his boots', was one remark I remember.

Nevertheless, Gimblett had a good season in 1936, and played the first two of his three Test matches; these were against India. If he had been playing in August as he had played in May, he must have had a very good chance of going with G. O. Allen's side to

Australia. That was an oddly chosen side, and one of its principal weaknesses was in opening batting. But Gimblett's was not the worst omission. Both Sutcliffe and Paynter were left at home, while in one Test Verity joined Barnett to open the innings (and they made the best England opening partnership of the series: fifty-three).

Gimblett played his third Test against the West Indies in 1939. You could not say that his Test career was unsuccessful (129 runs, average 32) but he did not play for his country again, though he was often near it. He was chosen as late as 1950 but withdrew through illness the day before the match. In those postwar years, it was difficult with Hutton and Washbrook present for other opening batsmen to get a look in.

But if his Test career was limited, he still holds three Somerset records: the most runs (23,007), the most centuries (50) and the highest score (310 not out). A useful life's work there. As he grew older, he became less of a dasher, unless the mood took him. It was not often, then, that we saw him use the hook, which had been one of his favourite strokes. I believe he reduced its use on the advice of Hammond, who was said to have taken the same decision for himself half a generation earlier. This was possibly a wiser decision for Hammond than for Gimblett, not just because Hammond was so good at all the other strokes, but because Gimblett, even more than most batsmen, liked to be in command, liked to be seen in command, never played better than when he *felt* in command: and the hook is a commanding stroke. It suited him.

Of the other prewar Somerset cricketers, I have mentioned Frank Lee, and his partnership of 234 with brother Jack at Leyton. I was interested to read in his autobiography (*Cricket, Lovely Cricket*, Stanley Paul, 1960) that they had taken their wives up to Leyton for the match. They were both Bath girls, for the brothers had settled in Bath. 'This naturally called for a celebration that evening with a dinner in town followed by a show – a truly happy and memorable day.' I find that a pleasing picture. I wonder what they went to see. I like to think it was *Badgers Green*, a happy country comedy with a cricketing touch, which must have been on about then.

But if I cannot recall the 234 partnership, I have a clear memory of another innings by Frank, against the Indians at Taunton in 1946. My father and I were driving down from Oxford to Devon and, as there was no particular hurry, decided to look in at the match for an hour or two. We arrived at about three in the afternoon and managed to get in, though the ground was packed, and I doubt if we would have done it had father not been wearing his clerical collar. We had to stand up to see at all. Lee and Gimblett were batting for Somerset. No wicket was down and the score was around sixty. Slow stuff it must have been, we thought, on such a fine day. Then we learnt from neighbours that the Indians had batted first, and Somerset had bowled them out for sixty-four. I know that this kind of story has often been told of spectators arriving late after an early collapse (Yorkshire's thirty-one at Huddersfield is an example). But father and I were certainly perplexed for a time at Taunton. Nor did Lee and Gimblett seem to be making much effort to get among the runs. They were not, I realise now, anxious to polish off the match in a couple of days, not with crowds so large as that. So we watched some dullish cricket, even Harold restraining himself, and no wicket had fallen when we departed. Still no luck with the tribe of Lee. Frank was, we later read, run out for 76 with the score 182. Somerset declared at more than 500 for 6. The Indians, who were a talented side that year, batted much better when they went in again. They often have made brave recoveries after being caught napping, or hopping, on a tricky English first morning pitch – but Somerset won by an innings, and I saw some of the later part of the match on my way back to Oxford.

M. M. Walford scored a century for Somerset. Micky Walford was a man with a natural gift for any kind of sport he chose to adopt, a triple Blue at Oxford, but much more than a talented games player. I joined him in some broadcasts in the following years, and was always impressed by his observation of the sporting scene. Yet he had to remain principally an observer, for most of his time was spent teaching, something I am sure he did very well. Yet he still liked to show he could play when he had the chance. There were grumbles in county sides at that period when, after the university match and the school term were over, professionals (many of them paid on a match basis) had to step down for the posh amateurs. I recall much wrath particularly among the professionals of Kent. But there were no grumbles in Somerset when Walford was available. In 1947 he scored nearly a thousand runs in the month of August, including 264 against Hampshire at Weston-super-Mare. I saw some of this innings. He had already made a lot of runs when I got there, and was flailing around. But his methods were usually orthodox, his technique sound. I also saw him bat on one of the ropier Somerset pitches, of which there were several – I think this one was at Wells – when he did not score very many, but studiously set himself to keep the opposition out until the game was safe.

Then there was Bertie Buse. He was a thoroughly good county cricketer, but did not stick in your memory, unless indeed you happened to meet him off the field in the evening behind a pint. In his early days he was, I think, conscious of his professional anonymity, compared with the Walfords and Gimbletts, and tried to counteract it by growing a sergeant-major moustache – an unusual thing for a cricketer in those days. When A. E. R. Gilligan first saw it, at Hove, he said, 'Who's that bloke, King Charles?' I cannot say that this remark strikes me as very funny, but Frank Lee and others present evidently thought it so.

The moustache was not the only soldierly thing about Buse. His bowling pace was what is called 'military medium', his batting was stiff but correct, there was something of the parade ground in his movements about the field. He was good enough to play county cricket regularly years before he did. He played as an amateur as early as 1929 when he was 19 years old. The trouble was that Somerset already had as many professionals as they could afford. He became professional to the Bath club instead (he also played Rugby for Bath, and Somerset at full-back – in those days the post of stern duty, the last line of defence). Although one always thinks of him as a Bath man, he was born in Bristol. However, in 1938 Somerset decided that they could manage to offer him a contract. He immediately took his place in the side, strengthened both the bowling and the middle-order batting, and his place, when fit, was never in doubt until his retirement in 1953.

He had a tragi-comic benefit match at Bath in 1953. Lancashire beat Somerset in a single day, and one of the chief reasons for this summary finish was that Buse had wasted no time in bowling Lancashire out. The Bath pitch then was not a good one. Brian Langford, I remember, began his successes there, and thought that first-class cricket must be the easiest game in the world. Buse sternly ticked him off one night over a beer or two: 'taking wickets here's like a pancake race at Midsomer Norton', was, I think, his phrase. Buse could be sometimes a little severe towards the younger men of the side, but they took it in good part for he was a respected man. I do not think Robertson-Glasgow ever wrote about him, which is a pity, but we have an admirable essay in David Foot's *From Grace to Botham* (The Redcliffe Press, 1980) from which I purloin this description of Buse's run-up to bowl:

> He started with a perfunctory walk as though he was taking a Sunday afternoon stroll along Great Pulteney Street. Then he offered a little medieval jig, hops of delicate, balletic balance, followed by a sudden, disconcerting acceleration. There still wasn't too much impetus by the time he reached the wickets but the ball was hurled down with the kind of thrust that revealed reserves of strength in those shoulder muscles.

He still lives and thrives at Bath, using up his spare time and energy as a messenger for the *Bath Chronicle*.

I shall only say a few words about J. C. White, because I wrote about him in a previous book (*The Cricket Captains of England*, Cassell, 1979). But I must not leave you with the impression that I have forgotten him. He is the only captain of England I have ever batted against. He had been at Taunton School, and used sometimes to revisit us and cast an eye over the youngsters in the nets, and it so happened that by the merest chance this white-haired, ruddy-faced old bean bowled a few balls to me. 'Mr White', we always called him, even when he was not present; never 'Jack' or 'Farmer' as the Somerset supporters did. He was a slow left-arm bowler, whose strength lay in flight rather than spin. He bore the burden of the English bowling during the Australian tour of 1928–9. 'Farmer' was not just a nickname. He was a real farmer, up in the Brendons, somewhere near Wiveliscombe. After he had retired from the captaincy of Somerset, he would return for the occasional match. Once he made an unexpected appearance late in the summer, and was seen to be in some difficulty in the field (although he could catch well, he had never been a whippet). 'Bit stiff', he confessed. 'First match for a month or two, I suppose?' said a sympathetic colleague. 'No', said Mr White, 'fell off top of haycart yesterday, ground's hard this time of year'.

And I must not forget Horace Hazell. I see him still on Somerset grounds, usually at Weston or Bath. To say 'he looks as young as ever' is not a conventional compliment, but a statement of fact. The truth is that Horace *never* looked young, and has in consequence the compensation of never looking old. He was J. C. White's successor in the side as slow left-arm bowler. He took 950 wickets for Somerset from the years 1929 to 1952.

He was born at Brislington, which you would describe today as a Bristol suburb. But it was undoubtedly in Somerset, according to the old boundaries (which county clubs still sensibly accept), though perilously near the Gloucestershire border. Brislington still has a useful cricket club. At least once Somerset played a Sunday match there, and Greg Chappell, a young man learning the English game with Somerset, scored a hundred runs. This was the first hundred ever made in a John Player match. Surrey scored 173 for 7, Somerset 175 for 1, with more than an over to spare, Chappell 128 not out. Jack Crapp, another man of whom I must write, lived in or near Brislington in the latter part of his life. I recall these details to make it clear to you that Brislington was a fit place for a Somerset cricketer to be born.

Horace was a tubby man, on the short side: not flabby, you understand – he could bowl long spells in the heat on plumb pitches without wilting – but plumpish. Near the end of his career, I was broadcasting commentary on a Gloucestershire/Somerset match at Bristol. It was Hammond's last match, and I shall refer to it again, but it is not Hammond with whom I am concerned now. Gloucestershire won the toss, Milton and Emmett batted, and were nearly 200 no wicket down. I and my number two (summariser) Michael Bowen agreed that Somerset's only hope lay in the new ball, in those days due after 200 runs had been scored. To our astonishment, the Somerset captain, a cheerful fair-haired Cambridge basher called Rogers, did not take the new ball, but kept Hazell on. Well, I was a young man, as commentators then went, and thought I knew more about the game than I did. I said I was baffled by the decision. Michael Bowen, who was also young though less dogmatic than I, concurred. Hazell then bowled Gloucestershire out, for not much more than 300. Collapse of stout commentators. Michael and I did not drink on the ground that evening (for in those days radio was still a kind of miracle, and players used to listen to us in the dressing rooms, chiefly in order to catch us out). We crept away to a nearby pub to share our consolatory pints.

I made another mistake in this match. Describing Hazell's approach, I said that 'he waddles up to the wicket'. I am not so sure, looking back, that the word was all that inappropriate: 'Like bias to the bowl, Which as more pond'rous, made its aim more true,

Obliquely waddling to the mark in view.' Pope, who wrote the lines, had not of course seen Hazell bowl, but it is not a bad description. I cannot claim, however, that I had Pope in mind when I used the term.

And now, young commentators, mark this. If you have used the wrong word or the unlucky phrase, forget it immediately and press on. On that occasion, I was conscious that 'waddles' was not the best choice, but harked back to it, embarrassedly saying, 'No, waddles is too unkind a word.' This drew every listener's attention to the fact that I had used it, and provoked a lot of irate correspondence from Somerset.

Horace did not turn the ball much, but kept a length. It took him some years to become established in the side, though he had, as R. A. Roberts wrote, 'all the attributes of his craft'. In 1936 he took eighty-seven wickets at twenty-one, twenty of them at Weston. He fell away for a couple of seasons, but in 1939 took five for six in Worcestershire's second innings at Kidderminster. This was a famous match which ended in a tie (Worcestershire 130 and 142, Somerset 131 and 141). Horace was last man out in Somerset's second innings. He was never much of a batsman, though capable of the sudden swish which might win a match at a crucial moment, or lose it.

After the war, he was a better bowler than before, a shade tubbier, but experience made up for that. In 1946, he took six for eighteen at Canterbury in Kent's first innings (eleven for fifty-two in the match), and also denied Gloucestershire a win at Bristol by putting on ninety-two for the last wicket with Buse. Somerset did not often win at Bristol in those days, but they were hard to beat. I remember another last wicket stand a few years later, when McMahon and Hilton, neither of them batsmen according to any-one's account but their own, held up a licks-lipping Gloucester-shire attack in the last three-quarters of an hour.

Ron Roberts felt that Hazell was not bowled enough. Of 1946, he says, 'Often, he did not go on until third or fourth change, whereas bowlers of similar type in other counties were used as first change. He bowled only 400 overs in the championship, and yet took 52 wickets at 17 runs each.' The Somerset captain then was Longrigg, later known as 'the silver-tongued solicitor' – a good chap, a good captain, but perhaps inclined to underestimate spin bowlers, because he played them so confidently himself, at least at Taunton with its short boundaries for the drive.

Since my narrative has bumped into Longrigg, I think he deserves a further paragraph or two. He was elegant in manners, in dress and in speech – a hard man to follow after dinner at a cricket gathering. He was close to Somerset cricket for fifty years, playing first for them in 1925, when still a schoolboy at Rugby (though he was born in Bath), and last in 1947. He was captain in 1938–9, and again in 1946. In the latter year he took them to fourth place in the championship, the highest they had been this century, and a very heartening season it was for Somerset. He was a left-hander, his instincts aggressive, though sometimes, especially when he was captain, he had to curb them in the interests of his side. But I have seen him hit sixes at Taunton – three in one afternoon before the war – of which Wellard would have been proud.

Wisden wrote of him after his death, aged 68, in 1974 (the obituary was anonymous, but it bears the stamp of my old friend Eric Hill) that 'he will be remembered for his unfailing courtesy, goodwill, and understanding, especially in some very heated county committee debates'. And my word, feelings did run high in Somerset cricket at times. Longrigg became both chairman and president of the club, and always decorated it. I still find myself looking round for him when I go there.

I must return to Horace. He topped the county averages in 1947, and took 100 wickets for the first time (it was really the first time he had been given the opportunity) in 1948. He took over 100 again in 1949, with 25 at Weston, and that year finished fourth in the national averages. He bowled 105 consecutive balls against Gloucestershire without conceding a run, and many of them to Tom Graveney. There were those who said then that Horace was the best slow left-hander in the country, and there was a case for him, as Bailey of Hampshire dropped into the background. But Horace, born in 1909, was only eighteen months younger than Bailey, and neither of them was ever seriously considered for an England side, though I remember John Arlott putting up an argument (with a touch of mischief in it) for Bailey to Walter Robins no less about 1948. I doubt if anyone ever put up even a mischievous argument for Horace. Apart from, or rather associated with, his figure, there was the fielding to be considered. He held them smartly at slip, but was not speedy when it came to a chase.

He still feels sad that his contract was not renewed at the end of the 1952 season, when he thought he still had a few more years left in him. He was, however, probably happier out of Somerset at that time when the committee meetings grew so heated. They finished bottom four years running. I remember, and indeed was peripherally involved in, the Somerset rumpuses of those years, and am bound to record my impression that most Somerset supporters greatly enjoyed them. To win a vote of no confidence in the committee was not, perhaps, so good as winning a match against Gloucestershire, but a tolerable winter substitute. Horace took no part in the arguments. He would nod his head and drink his bottle of Bass as his friends told him about them. You must not think of him, though, as unconversational. He is a good man with a story, though not always to be trusted when it comes to his batting recollections. It is true that once he hit Verity for 28 runs in an over, at Bath, and scored more than 2000 runs during his career, but his average was just over 8.

After he had left the first-class game, Horace played for some time in the Birmingham League with Mitchell and Butler's (this must have given pain to such a devoted a Bass man), and did some coaching. The name Hazell is a fairly frequent one in Somerset (you may remember a fine Rugby forward, David Hazell, from Taunton School, a few years back). I heard someone say, watching Horace sauntering round the ground recently, 'Ah, there goes the old oil of Hazell.' I thought for a moment it was an American joke. Then I remembered: 'oil of hazel', according to the *Shorter Oxford*, is 'a jocular name for an oil alleged to be contained in a green hazel rod, and to be the efficacious element in a sound drubbing'. (I had a touch of something of the kind myself, not far from the Taunton ground.) Well, there it is. Horace kept his oil going jocularly for a long time, and sometimes his rod would produce unexpected drubbings for unsuspecting batsmen.

These were some of the Somerset cricketers who drew my youthful attention. But I had no sense of identification with the west of England – it was simply where I went to school – nor the least thought that I should spend the rest of my life there.

IV
'An Emperor . . .'

'Antipodites have their feete downwards,
and their heads upwards, as well as wee.'
Melton

It was postwar Oxford which gave me the chance of watching first-class cricket regularly since the Leyton days. When I go to the Parks nowadays (admittedly it always seems to be cold and wet in early May) I find that hardly anyone watches the cricket. In the afternoon there will be a small group huddled around the beer tent, if the beer tent has bothered to open, or it has even occurred to anyone to put it up. That will be about all, except for citizens walking their dogs (the Parks is public territory, no charge for admission) who sometimes watch a couple of overs while the dogs are about their business. Fenner's is less beautiful than the Parks, scenically (despite the blows the Parks have suffered from Dutch elm bugs) but incomparably better organised when it comes to looking after spectators.

Yet in the years just after the war, there was always a big crowd in the Parks when the university was playing, even if the weather was doubtful. The general idea among students then, before lectures had become a fetish, was to read in the morning and the evening and take the afternoon off. Oxford were a good side in those years – good enough to have come in the top half of the county championship. The average age was high, because so many had been delayed by the war. We were a bit short on bowling, as university sides usually are against canny professionals working for their places, but the batting was strong. Our pride and joy was Martin Donnelly.

Donnelly was a batsman of the highest class, whose reputation does not shine so brightly as it should. This is partly because the war took away so much of his career, and partly because his one comparatively unsuccessful season in England coincided with the visit of the Australians in 1948. Australians never had the chance of seeing Donnelly at his best. This was a pity, because his style was based on the best Australian methods. He had certain similarities with Bradman: the build, the hawkeye, the forcing stroke off the toes square with the wicket on the leg side, the determination to establish a psychological supremacy over the bowler at once. Once Gloucestershire won the toss at Oxford and put the university in. It was bound to be a spinner's pitch, and Tom Goddard was genially rubbing his large hands (this is not a piece of poetic invention: I can see him rubbing them now, as he walked down the steps of the tiny pavilion). Donnelly responded by going in first, not his usual position. After a few perfunctory overs by Whomever and Whichever, who opened the bowling for Gloucestershire for so many years until the shine was off for the spinners, Tom came on. Donnelly set about him. We had an hour or so of gripping cricket, before Donnelly was caught on the boundary, after scoring seventy trying to hit Tom straight for a second consecutive six.

I have risked comparing him with Bradman, but you will see from that episode that he did not share Bradman's determination *never* to get out. And Donnelly was left handed. Perhaps Clem Hill or, later, Neil Harvey, would be the nearest Australian equivalents.

Donnelly first came to England in 1937, with M. L. Page's New Zealand team. New Zealand were not strong that year, but had three outstanding players: Cowie, the fast bowler (who would have won the second Test had his fieldsmen held their catches) and the young batsmen Wallace and Donnelly. Donnelly was then 19 years old, and during the tour scored 1400 runs, average 37. *Wisden* called him – a characteristic *Wisden* phrase – 'a star in the making', and went on, more informatively: 'He showed remarkable coolness at a crisis, one memorable instance of this being in the Test match at Lord's, where he and Kerr successfully baulked England's efforts to win, and Donnelly emphasised his assurance by some skilful hooking of the fast bowling.' Donnelly scored twenty-one, and was out to the last ball of the match. The fast bowlers were Gover and Voce. 'His assurance', his 'skilful hooking' – to those of us who saw him in later years, the words have a familiar ring.

Back in New Zealand, Donnelly scored many runs in the Plunket

Shield competition, but the next the English cricket public heard of him was in 1945. Stationed over here, he played in the tremendous game that year between England and the Dominions at Lord's, which must have been one of the best cricket matches ever played. The Dominions scored 307 (Donnelly 133, Pepper 51, Wright 5 for 90). Donnelly, who scored 86 of his runs in boundaries, went in at number five and was last out. England scored 287 (Hammond 121). The Dominions then scored 336 (Miller 185; Wright 5 for 105; Donnelly 29; Constantine – the captain – 40). Miller and Constantine put on 117 in 40 minutes, and one of Miller's seven sixes nearly went over the pavilion. People who had seen both hits declared that Miller's was just as big as Albert Trott's but that since the time of Trott there had been additional building on the roof, which caused Miller's to bounce back and lodge on top of the broadcasting box. England had to make 357 in 270 minutes, and while Hammond (102) was in looked as if they might get them, but were beaten in the end by 45 runs with ten minutes to spare.

I did not see this match. But to recall it even now stirs the imagination. Such names! Hammond, Miller, Wright, Constantine, Donnelly . . . Hassett was to have captained the Dominions eleven, but when he was unfit, the captaincy was offered to Constantine as the senior man. Obvious enough, you would think, but at that time it caused some tremors. After all, here were the representatives of the Dominions being led out at Lord's by, well, not to put too fine a point about it, by what you could only call, taking it by and large, a *black* man . . . The Dominions eleven were not in the least surprised nor concerned. Learie took it in his gentle stride, feeling, as Winston felt when invited to form a government, that it was much the best plan.

Donnelly's play in this match and others that season made it clear that the prophecy of 1937 was right, and that a great batsman was with us. Oxford's expectation was high, and in the two years he spent with us was not disappointed. I saw, I think, at least part of every innings he played in the Parks in 1946. He began with thirty-five and twenty-five against Gloucestershire. It was, as I have described, not the last time he underestimated Tom Goddard. Many overseas players of that period could not bring themselves to believe that off-spinners on English pitches needed to be treated with care. He then scored 61 and 116 not out (in two hours) against that good Indian side, and followed with 139 and 95 against

Lancashire. If the hit which got him out in his second innings had carried for six – it only needed another yard or so – he would have scored the fastest hundred of the season. By this time town as well as gown hurried to the Parks, whenever it seemed likely that Donnelly would be batting. He scored 1256 runs for the university that season, average 63, finishing with 142 against Cambridge, an innings which settled the match. Not improbably with nothing at stake in the second innings he was out for one.

In 1947 he was Oxford's captain. He did not beat Cambridge that year, though the side was probably stronger than that of 1946: Pawson, Keighley, Mallett, Kardar, Maudsley, Whitcombe (a very tall fast bowler who would probably have played for England, given the state of English fast bowling at that time, had he been able to stay in the game). There was also H. B. Robinson, an off-spinner, whom I saw years later captaining Canada at Scarborough. Players as good as B. H. Travers and M. A. Sutton, both Blues, had to be left out. Donnelly scored 1144 runs at an average of 67. Oxford won five first-class matches, and only two were lost. It seemed as if the Cambridge match was well in hand, but after they had followed on, T. E. Bailey took root and saved the match as he has done so many others since. Donnelly made up for this disappointment to some extent by scoring 162 for the gentlemen against the players. He was not out, and he batted for three hours. Many who saw the innings have said that it was the best played for the gentlemen since the first war, and remained so right up to the abolition of the fixture. An interesting by-product of this season was that Kardar, who had toured with the 1946 Indians as a batsman and occasional fast bowler, became on Donnelly's advice a slow left-hand spinner with notable results.

In this year, 1947, I was the cricket correspondent of *Isis*, at that time the leading university magazine. I was paid £4 for the term's work, which was a lot of money. Although I had edited *The Tauntonian*, and written reports of school matches (sometimes submitting them to *The Times*, and even getting one or two published unpaid), this was the first time I ever became a professional cricket writer. I enjoyed more than the money, the pleasure of sitting in the pavilion ostentatiously taking notes, and holding forth in the common room in the evenings with all the authority of my position. I did not dare to use the press box. This seems to me strange looking back, because I was a cocky young man, but I didn't. I was rather scared of those impressive gentlemen who sat there, brushing their moustaches, representing *The Oxford Mail*, *The Daily Telegraph* (heavens, could it be Swanton?) and even, strictly anonymously of course, the man from *The Times*.

I suppose this helped to form a habit, for I have never been much of an enthusiast for press boxes. There is so much clatter in them – necessarily so, with all those typewriters and telephones. There is frequently a bore who spends the day telling everybody his latest dirty stories. It is hard to concentrate on the play. Of course it is a help to have colleagues handy for checking doubtful points, but because I was for many years a broadcaster rather than a journalist, I grew used to watching from a separate commentary point, alone or with just one companion. You had to make your own mistakes, and this is probably the best training, provided that you do not make them too often.

One of my *Isis* reports has survived. Oxford had been outplayed by Lancashire, and on the third day had nothing to hope for but a draw, which they achieved. Here is my account of Donnelly's innings. You will see that my style was, to put it kindly, unformed: three whacking clichés in the first two sentences.

> We watched with bated breath while Roberts wheeled up over after tempting over outside the off-stump. Donnelly was proof against his wiles. Oxford must not lose the match; and that meant, in effect, that he must not get out. Now and then a loose ball – or one that could reasonably be pretended to be such – went to the boundary. The runs came along at a rate slightly faster than the normal scoring pace in first-class cricket – that is to say, about half as fast as Donnelly usually makes them. It was a remarkable example of calculated restraint – the one attribute of batsmanship that we have sometimes thought he lacked. And it was never dull.

Donnelly reached his century, in this restrained innings, in 139 minutes. At the end he was 154 not out. The bowlers were Phillipson, Pollard, Garlick and Roberts. Pollard had already played for England and was to do so again. Phillipson was thought to be close to the England side, and Roberts knowingly talked about as a coming spinner. It was not a negligible attack.

Donnelly used to wear a curious cap. It was rather too large for him, coloured in stripes of soiled maroon and sour milk, and shaped like a shopping basket. Much argument went on round the ring about its derivation. We ultimately discovered that he had bought it during the war at a Cairo bazaar.

He had that one disappointing season, 1948. Down from Oxford, and employed by Courtauld's of Coventry, he appeared in about half Warwickshire's matches, but only averaged thirty-two. He played for MCC against the Australians at Lord's, scoring five and sixteen. He did, however, end with a flourish – 208 not out for MCC against Yorkshire at Scarborough.

He had, perhaps, been saving his concentration for the New Zealand tour of England in 1949. It was known that this would be his last full season in first-class cricket. On that tour he scored 2287 runs, average nearly 62, and in the Tests scored 462, average 77. This was, I think, the best New Zealand side we have had over here. They were slightly miffed at being awarded only four three-day Tests, and decided that whatever else happened they were not going to be beaten. Nor were they – four drawn matches – but you must not imagine from that that they played dully. Their batting order began Sutcliffe, Scott, Hadlee, Wallace, Donnelly, Reid, and not many sides have had a better first six. They were short of bowlers, except for the aging Cowie and an accurate though not penetrating slow left-hander, Burtt.

Donnelly scored 206 at Lord's, completing a rare and prized triple, centuries in the university match, for the gentlemen and in a Lord's Test. He was top of the New Zealand averages. Possibly the needs of his side caused him to curb his stroke play a little. *Wisden* reports that Sutcliffe was the more 'brilliant' batsman, but adds 'Responsibility at no time caused (Donnelly) to be ultra-careful; it did serve to make him even harder to dismiss than before, and against him bowlers could seldom have viewed their prospects with optimism.'

It was a memorable season for him and for his country. But that, alas! was more or less the end of his cricketing career. The 1949 New Zealanders lost only one match, at Oxford of all places. I had gone down from Oxford by then, and did not see much of Donnelly that season, but I did see the second day of the Oxford match. Donnelly was cheered all the way to the wicket, but was caught from a skier to short-leg before he had scored. He had been held back to number six, because the New Zealanders had been in trouble the night before on a wet pitch. Oxford sensed they had a chance of winning. Even so, there was as much pain as pleasure in the cry of the crowd when he was out.

At the end of that day, New Zealand had bowled Oxford out for 72, but still needed 164 to win, with 5 second innings wickets down. Donnelly and Wallace (Sutcliffe was not playing) had been held back in the order again, and on the third morning joined in an eighth-wicket partnership which looked as if it might swing the match. But Donnelly was bowled, playing on to Kardar, whom he had urged to take up spin bowling: a case of *mine own executioner*. Oxford won by eighty-three runs.

Sutcliffe was a very good batsman, and I am pleased to say I saw him score many runs, and came to know him quite well on later visits to England (a capital man for a Rugby song), but I never thought him so good as Donnelly. I would put Donnelly without hesitation into a 'best eleven' limited to cricketers I have seen. Put that down to university partisanship if you wish.

Certainly we were keen about Oxford cricket at that time. Senior and junior members of the university were constantly looking in at the Parks for free cricket. If you occupy a seat nowadays you have to pay for it, and even if you stand you are likely to be confronted politely by a contributions box. A few years ago the box was often carried by the Oxford coach, Arthur Milton, looking as pink and youthful as any undergraduate. 'I think it's a bit hard', he would say disarmingly, 'having to preach the sermon *and* take the collection.'

There is not often much money in the box today. It is customary to put this down to the increased demands of the examiners, but this is not, in my view, an adequate explanation. Examinations do account for the university eleven being frequently below strength during term. A man facing final schools can hardly be expected to make a public display of staying away from his books. But are your potential undergraduate spectators so devoted to academic duty, so passionately set on a good degree, that they cannot spare time to watch for an hour or two around lunchtime or the early evening? Of course not. Look at all the other extra-curricular activities they undertake. The truth is, they have simply lost interest. I know that there are obsessions with lectures and seminars as the way to a degree, rather than with reading. The advantage of 'reading' for a degree is that you can do it when you like – provided you do enough of it.

I do not wish it to be thought from these remarks that I ally myself with those who think universities exist for sporting activities. I do not think that exceptional athletic ability should be a qualification for admission to Oxford or Cambridge or anywhere else. There were far too many healthy dunderheads at Oxford in my time.

Not that Martin Donnelly was one of them: a very bright young man, as his subsequent career demonstrated. Something I have not mentioned about him, because I suppose we took it for granted, was his sportsmanship. He would give himself out, or 'walk' as the phrase now goes. At an early stage of his big innings in the 1946 university match, he thought he had been stumped and promptly turned away towards the pavilion (the bowling was from the Nursery end). He did this tranquilly, unostentatiously, though it was a heart-stopping moment for Oxford supporters. When he realised that the square-leg umpire had given him not out, he as tranquilly returned. It was his view that matters such as stumpings and lbw decisions were better judged by the umpire, but a catch at the wicket was often a difficult decision for the umpire, and the batsman (he maintained) invariably knew whether he had hit the ball or not. I doubt if in all his playing days he allowed himself to be given 'not out' to a catch at the wicket which he knew ought to be 'out'. In 1947, when he was the fielding captain at Chichester, he recalled A. P. Doggart to the wicket, when Doggart had been given out leg-before after playing the ball. He did these things so graciously that no umpire could take offence.

Donnelly was also a rugby player. Some years ago, I met a New Zealander in a train, and mentioned what a marvellous player I thought Donnelly was. 'Yes', said the New Zealander, a shade dubiously, 'but a better five-eighths than a full-back'. When I said that it was Donnelly's cricket that I had in mind, he said 'New Zealanders can't play cricket'. This was the belief of most New Zealanders then, an inhibition which did much for many years to stop them winning Test matches. I remember that their 1958 side – not a good one, caught in a bad summer – losing four by large margins and scrambling a draw in the fifth, preceded a visit by the All Blacks. There was a newspaper cartoon (I am sorry I cannot remember by whom) of a very big rugby player stepping off the boat, tapping on the shoulder a diminutive cricket player departing, and saying, 'Don't worry, son. We'll put that right'.

Donnelly played full-back for Oxford against the Kiwis in 1945; fly-half against Cambridge in 1946; and in the centre on the one occasion he was chosen to play for England. It was at fly-half, outside Newton-Thompson, that he touched heights comparable to those he climbed in cricket. It was absurd that he and Newton-Thompson were never chosen for England as a half-back pair. Oxford's 1946 rugby side, unbeaten in Michaelmas term, was probably the best to win the university match since the second war. Oxford were possibly a better side under Willcox, and Cambridge in 1957 better still: but both those sides unexpectedly lost at Twickenham.

Donnelly's batting had one quirk. He did not bother about the quick single. Practically all his runs came in boundaries, or leisurely pushes for one. His belief was that once he had determined to hit a ball, it should go for four or six (though, like Bradman, he hit relatively few sixes). If it did not go to the boundary, it was not worth more than one. This caused some slight embarrassment when he had to bat with H. A. Pawson, who was the fastest man between the wickets I have ever seen. It delighted the Parks to see Pawson halfway down on his third run while Donnelly was deciding it was not worth embarking on a second. The girlish screams, about equally divided as to whether it was darling Martin's fault or dear Tony's, must have shaken choral evensong at Keble. But I do not actually remember them finishing up at the same end.

A word or two about some of the other Oxford cricketers of that time: Tony Pawson has remained a lifelong friend, one of those friends you may not meet very often, but are delighted when you do, picking it up just where you left off. I first met him in the buttery at Queen's, Oxford. He was already iron-grey, and rather solemn looking, despite his gaiety between wickets. I rather think looking back that his heart was in fishing (at which he has often represented England). But he was a batsman good enough to have played for England had he decided to give time to it, and had England been less rich with batsmen. He captained Oxford after Donnelly went down, and scored a century at Lord's in a convincing win. He was also an excellent soccer player. He turned out once with remarkable success for Charlton Athletic – then in the first division. He had much to do with that strange anachronism, Pegasus, the Oxford/Cambridge combination which two years running won the FA Amateur Cup. He has written an enchanting book about these and other experiences (*Runs and Catches*, Faber, 1980). In this he told what was to me a new cricket story. New cricket stories are rare, though the names change. This concerned Rockley Wilson, who played for Yorkshire and England in the 1920s, and taught Pawson cricket at Winchester. Wilson was a schoolmaster who was not troubled

> 'about making remarks which were regarded as of questionable taste in those more modest days. When a boy unknown to him was assigned to his net and began bowling with wild abandon he called: "What's your name, young man?"
> "Badcock, sir."
> "Don't think much of your balls, either." '

Then there was R. H. Maudsley, Donnelly's principal stay at the other end in 1946. He won another Blue in 1947, but could not play much that season because of examinations, something he took very seriously. Later he played for Warwickshire, of whom he was joint captain with Tom Dollery in 1948. He was just the kind of batsman any university side longs for nowadays: large, fearless, unruffled, solid. In 1946 he averaged thirty-six for Oxford. He took a first in law, taught at his college, Brasenose, and held a chair at King's College, London, and later at the New York Law School. I lost touch with him, though shortly before his death in 1981 I met him at the Parks, and we had some good talk about the 1946 and 1947 Oxford sides. He was, I thought, unduly proud of his bowling, which I scarcely remembered, except that it was medium pace and vaguely swinging. But he did take, as he emphasized, six for fifty-four at the Oval against Surrey, bowling unchanged with Eric Hollies.

Finally, I will put in a word for a cricketer of whom few of you will have heard, Geoffrey Beck. Geoffrey won a wartime Blue for Oxford, and in fact scored two sixties (in one-day matches) at Lord's within a week. He should certainly have been chosen for Oxford in 1946 when the side was a batsman short. He had to be brought in because of injuries on tour, and promptly scored fifty against Surrey. But he was not chosen for Lord's. They filled up the side with rugby Blues, members of Vincent's, the lads. Geoffrey was a quiet man, studying for the Congregational ministry at Mansfield, well enough liked but certainly not one of the lads. I do not think he ever played first-class cricket again, which was a waste, though I doubt if it worried him as he proceeded successfully in his chosen career. But if I am inclined to romanticise Oxford cricket, I remember Geoffrey, and that there was the snobby, toffee-nosed side to it. He must have been pleased, even with a touch of rue, that Mansfield has made such a powerful sporting contribution in recent years.

V
'...and Some Clowns'

How doth the little crocodile
Improve his shining tail
Carroll

A quality of cricket has been what might be called its casual sides, or fun sides. They are not incapable of taking a game seriously, but their purpose is to enjoy it, irrespective of the result. Most cricketers have been associated with such organisations at one time or another, and everyone naturally thinks his own the best, so I have no hesitation in putting in a claim for the Oxford Crocodiles, which flourished for a few years after the second war, on tours of the west.

The genesis of the Crocodiles was a more long standing institution: The Queen's College (Oxford) Imperial Quondams Cricket Club, to give its full majestic name. I knew it, and indeed was its captain at one time. The Quondams, who played against villages near Oxford, consisted mostly of men in their finals year, who could not give time to the serious business of the college first eleven; or of men who were not good enough to play for the college second eleven but could not resist the game. Sometimes an aging don might play, sometimes a man who had scarcely played cricket at all but had social merits: you know the kind of mixture – it usually meant that we had three or four pretty good cricketers and the rest cheerful rabbits.

The Quondams had been founded, I understood, in the early 1930s. This was not correct, as I learnt from a large correspondence when once I wrote about them in *The Times*, but for now I tell the tale as I was told. Our first president we believed was D. G. Bradman, who, when invited, wrote a polite letter of acceptance. Later it was proposed, for reasons now obscure, that the Emperor Hirohito should be made president. A compromise was reached, and it was decided that Bradman and Hirohito should hold the office jointly. The emperor also wrote a polite letter of acceptance, and thus the word 'Imperial' was included in the club's title.

After the war, it was suggested that the emperor should be struck from the roll. I am glad to say that the Quondams rejected this racialist proposition, on the grounds that the joint-president had suffered much, and needed no further public humiliation. Indeed, instead we passed a resolution condoling with him on the loss of his godhead. Again, a polite note was received from Tokyo. I trust these documents are still preserved. They certainly existed once.

The Crocodiles (so called, a feeble enough joke, because they always had a long tail) worked on much the same principles as the Quondams, though mostly a touring side. Several men were members of both, but the Crocodiles were not confined to Queensmen. The standard of play was higher though still eccentric. We did much to improve the profits of various West Country inns. Our president was M. P. Donnelly, and once, in a warming-up match near Oxford, he actually played for us, though he did not bat because it rained. I remember our first two matches on our first tour. We began with an evening match at Buckfastleigh in Devon. I greeted Crocodiles (for I lived at Totnes, nearby) off a series of afternoon trains (there is still a lovely little line there, run by the Dart Valley company). Many of them had come far. It was a hot day; all were perspiring and thirsty. The Buckfastleigh ground, a beautiful one, is, or was, high on a plateau, and at the bottom of the hill which approaches it is, or was, a pub. The pub opened at five, and the match did not begin until half-past six. They decided with one accord that, since they were in Devon, the correct drink was cider. I did my best to warn them, having suffered myself, that scrumpy had daemonic properties, but they were young men from Oxford, many of whom had served in the war, and were confident they could handle any sort of drink. At about six o'clock, I led my side, who encouraged themselves by song, up the hill. The average consumption had been, I should think, four and a half pints. My heart did not lift when I saw a poster advertising the match as 'Buckfastleigh v. Oxford University', and that Donnelly (whose name was on our notepaper) would be playing. We were also two men short, though whether they had missed the trains or had stayed with the scrumpy I was not sure. None of this perturbed the happy band of brothers. The only thing to do was to win the toss, put the others in and give the cider a chance to wear off. I lost the toss and we were put in. Laughing and smiling, the Crocodiles approached the wicket, and swiftly, laughing even more heartily, departed from it. We were all out for twenty-six, and though we took a few wickets, it was an ignominious defeat. The local paper reported 'OXFORD CRACKS SHATTERED'. They remembered this against me at Buckfastleigh for years. When I played rugby there, or even if I preached there in the chapel, somebody was sure to bring it up.

The next day we had to play a full-scale match at Torquay. Very posh, Torquay; blimey, they had scorecards, and C. V. G. Haines was their captain. Haines had been playing a good deal for Glamorgan that season, and at the time – I promise this is true – was head of the first-class batting averages, with a figure of about eighty. This was such an alarming prospect that I wondered if I could get the side there at all. On the way there we lost M. J. Kalyasunderam, who I believe diffidently paid his entrance fee to get in. Kalyasunderam was an admirable tourist, none better with an Indian lullaby after dinner, but not a commanding batsman. It was in this match that he scored a four to long-leg, driving towards mid-off (his most prolific stroke) and I heard a Torquay colonel, presumably remembering Ranji, say in all seriousness 'Marvellous eyes these eastern fellows have'.)

We lost the toss. After Torquay had scored about forty we took a wicket, and the dreaded Haines came in. I decided that this was the time for a bit of dashing captaincy, and brought on Bill Howarth (now professor of French at Bristol University). We really only had two chaps who could bowl at all, and they had done their best. Bill announced he was an off-spinner, and certainly looked very impressive with a green cap – the Australian sort that bulges over the ears. He insisted on a deep backward square-leg. The duty fell on Jimmy Craig, who is, as I write, our ambassador in Jeddah. Jimmy was our wicket-keeper, and it was a long time since he had fielded anywhere else, but though we had now increased our numbers to ten, we had had to ask Torquay for a player. The one they offered would only play if he kept wicket, so Jimmy had been dispatched to pastures new.

Haines had scored one and Bill began to bowl at him. His first ball was a long hop, but it turned, yes, it turned, and Haines, hitting a little too early, sent it high and fiercely towards deep backward square-leg. Bill insists to this day that he deceived him in the flight. We imagined that it would clear the ground, but Jimmy Craig stood there steadfastly, though I would not have blamed him had he quietly turned his back and walked away to look up some intricate diplomatic point in the public library. But he stood there like a man, and caught it. It really was a devil of a good catch, as Sir James Craig recently confirmed to me by diplomatic bag from Jeddah. From that moment, the Crocodiles became a cricket team. We lost, but got them out for about 180, and were not far behind at the end. Indeed, when Basil Wigoder and Jeremy Potter (yes, two more familiar names) were making a stand for the third wicket, we looked like winning it. The local paper said 'STUDENTS SHAKE TORQUAY'. Much better.

The same pattern continued while the Crocodiles lasted. We were, on a small scale, rather like Somerset, doing well against strong sides and poorly against what were supposed to be weak ones. There was a match against Haytor Vale, who had a saucer-shaped ground in the Dartmoor foothills. The square was well cut, but once off that you found the grass round your knees. We got them out fairly cheaply, thanks to the bowling of A. W. Dodds (now vicar of Chedworth, a canon, rural dean of Northleach and brother of T. C. Dodds of Essex, of whom I shall have more to say). But our batting also collapsed, and with an over to go it was clear that we could not win the match but had to save it. Our last man in was P. J. Hilton. I don't know where Peter is now; he was a mathematician of exceptional brilliance. After holding several senior professorial positions in England, he became part of the brain drain to America. Reading C. P. Snow on G. H. Hardy made me think that Hardy and Hilton were much of a kind: both drawn to cricket, neither with any particular talent for it. Peter certainly had not played much before his appearance at Haytor Vale when he had to save the match. We had been talking the usual stuff about 'keeping the bat in the blockhole'. Peter, with a few swift calculations, decided that the best place to keep the bat, if the object was to prevent the ball hitting the wicket, was 17.4 (or something) inches outside the crease. He measured the distance, placed his bat there, stretching out his back leg so that he could not be stumped. He knew that the danger was that he might, at the last moment, be tempted to hit the ball, so he directed his gaze firmly towards first slip. It was some time before the bowler could be persuaded to bowl. Five times did the ball smack on Peter's unrelenting bat. I wish this story had a happy ending. The last ball of the match just nudged the bat's shoulder, and Peter was caught at slip, to which position his eyes were still devotedly fixed.

In the next match he used a different theory. He had one ball and hit it for six – a whacker which won the match. In the match after that, as he was about to go in, a fellow mathematician asked of him 'Is it the static or the dynamic today?'

We were young men, whose evening conversations alternated between the earnest and the bawdy, as young men's conversations must always have done. There was one evening when solemnly someone quoted some lines from William Watson. Watson was rather old hat even then, but as George Sampson wrote was, 'at his best, a poet of fine vision with a command of sonorous language'. Someone (I can't remember who, but it was not I) said:

> *Ah! but the apparition, the dumb sign,*
> *The beckoning finger, bidding us forego*
> *The fellowship, the laughter and the wine,*
> *The friends, the festal glow.*
> *And Ah to know not, while with friends we sit,*
> *And while the purple joy is passed about,*
> *Whether 'tis ampler day, divinelier lit,*
> *Or homeless night without.*

There was a stillness. We sound a pompous and precious lot, but most of these men had fought at D-day, or flown over Germany, or sailed against hopeless odds in the Java seas. They had often asked themselves, even half-curiously, whether ampler day or homeless night lay ahead of them.

But in a minute or two we were back discussing the follies of the England selectors, and Harold Gardiner (later a master at Bedales, and as good at an English song as Kalyasunderam was with an Indian one) would be beginning 'There was an old farmer ...'

Gone, long gone, are the Crocodiles, at least in their Crocodilean aspects. We do, some of us, meet occasionally, and do not think that the England selectors have improved much. The Quondams have survived (my two eldest sons have both been members). After I wrote about them in *The Times*, I received several indignant letters from Quondams of the 1920s, saying that my description of their origins was incorrect. Apparently the real founder was John Bell, dean of the college, and later high master of St Paul's. I also learnt that the Crocodiles have a successor, known as the Philippics, after Queen Philippa, from whom the college was named (she was the one, you remember, who begged off the burghers of Calais). Mr J. R. Steele of Beckenham sent me an account of their doings, of which at least this paragraph seems to me worth reproducing: the tone was set he says:

> by the first game of the first tour, at Barnard Castle. We had hired two old Austin 6's. [The Crocodiles hired an ancient 13-seater Chevrolet coach in 1946 – A.G.] There was no argument about the drivers since only two of us had licences. The cars had to be started on the handle and the effort on the first morning had rubbed the skin from the fingers of our opening bowler, one A. H. Cooper, a rugby Blue whose bowling was noted more for its vigour than its skill. Gallant as ever, he bowled the first over, but decided at the end of it that his hand needed medication. The other opening bowler, D. Urquhart bowled four balls at brisk pace, pulled a muscle and finished the over bowling slow off-spinners. The first bowling change took place after two overs (a replacement for Cooper) and the second after three (a replacement for Urquhart). By the end of the fourth over, Cooper was back with his hand covered in lint and sticking plaster. A third bowling change was therefore made after four overs (the return of Cooper). Unfortunately, when he bowled the first ball of his new spell the ball stuck to the sticking plaster on his hand, and instead of moving rapidly and approximately in the direction of the batsman, went behind him and struck mid-on rather sharply on the shin. The fourth bowling change therefore took place after six overs . . .

Ah, that is the spirit, and I am sorry I never had the chance to utter a philippic with Messrs Steele, Cooper and Urquhart. But as I began by saying, every man has his own touring side, and gone, long gone, are the Quondam Crocodiles, and our nice hand-made flag with the crocodile stitched upon it, with its thirsty red tongue and its long tail. It must be some time since any of us seriously put bat to ball. But, lord! we had some fun.

VI

A Touch More Scrumpy

'Somerset is a worthy county, though damp,
full of zeal and husbandry'.

Johnson

I came down from Oxford in 1947. My homes since then have
been in the west – after Cornwall, Devon, then Gloucestershire,
now Somerset (taking no notice of the new-fangled 'Avon'). Most
of the first-class cricket I saw in the next decade was in the west. I
still supported Yorkshire against everybody, but it did not take
long for my affection for Somerset and Gloucestershire to grow.
There was a time when I might even have preferred Somerset or
Gloucestershire to beat Yorkshire – not now, mind, not in 1984,
when Yorkshire have had such lengthy, unprecedented troubles.
Even when Yorkshire were still winning championships, I found
my heart was instinctively with the white rose when I was actually
present at a match. Another relic of my early upbringing is that
I cannot help liking to see Lancashire lose. In this I differ from my
friend and fellow Yorkshireman Don Mosey, who, if Yorkshire
does not win, likes Lancashire to. I was brought up to believe that
the best thing was a Yorkshire victory; and the second best thing a
Lancashire defeat.

I first broadcast about cricket in 1948, assisted by Arlott and
Andrews in that Australian match at Taunton. This was not a
commentary, except for the audition, just an evening report for
'Sport in the West'. At that time I was a member of the staff of the
University College of the South West, Exeter (as it then was), and
the occasional broadcast was a useful way of helping out a meagre

salary. The following year, unexpectedly, and not of my own initiative, I joined the staff of the BBC at Plymouth, as what was called a 'general programme assistant'. This turned out to mean, principally, a talks and features producer, something I enjoyed very much. But I had to give up cricket commentary. As the BBC was run then, staff were not supposed to do the actual broadcasting themselves. I stayed on the staff for five years, and although towards the end of this time I was asked to do cricket and rugby commentaries occasionally, this was simply on the basis of helping out, not because it was part of my job, or because I was thought specially good at it. However, when I decided to try my luck as a freelance, commentary came in useful, and gradually developed into a regular, if minor, source of income. The West of England Home Service (so shamefully abolished by the London mandarins in the early 1970s) covered a great deal of cricket in those days: all matches in which Gloucestershire, Somerset, or Hampshire were playing one another; and their matches against touring sides; and (in collaboration with the Welsh Home Service) their matches against Glamorgan; and any other matches which seemed interesting in the light of their championship positions.

Very little cricket commentary is done today, apart from 'Test Match Special'. The commentator on, say 'Sport on Two', on Saturday afternoons, is lucky if he gets more than a minute at a time. The requirements of a short report ('one minute fifteen please and may I have your outcue') and a twenty-minute stint are so different that skill at one almost demands clumsiness at the other. But I do not wish to become involved in a discussion of BBC policy. I merely point out how different it was then. I remember once beginning a commentary on the first day of Hampshire v. somebody at 11.30 on the first day, and continuing until 12.15, no scorer, no number two. During this time Rogers and Gray scored eight runs, all in singles. I felt some relish afterwards that I had got through it without breaking down, but it cannot have made compelling listening.

John Arlott was the senior commentator in the west, as he was to become in England (Hampshire was always included in the west region because of the positioning of the transmitters). But he was often away on Tests and other major occasions, and so I found myself with quite a lot of humble county matches to do, and sometimes other regions would ask me to help them out. This amounted after a few years to perhaps thirty or forty days of cricket a season. It was 1962, fourteen years after that first effort at Taunton, before I was thought good enough to be given a Test match.

Here is a reflection. When my cricket was limited to thirty days a season, I was perplexed by the attitude of some – indeed, most – of the county cricketers I met. They did not seem to enjoy playing cricket nearly so much as I enjoyed broadcasting about it. When it came to early August, they would say comfortingly to one another that there was not long to go. This rather shocked me. Here were these people living, surely, the best and happiest of lives, getting paid for it, only working five months or so in the year, and yet they grew tired and bored! When years later I found myself (largely by accident) reporting cricket all through the season, sometimes seven days a week, I saw the cricketers' point. Instead of rising in the morning with a cheerful 'Hurray! Cricket to-day!' my waking thought would be 'Hell, cricket again.' Cricket is a time-consuming game, and requires fairly continuous concentration and long hours of travel. I do my travelling whenever I can by train: and a train journey from, for instance, Bristol to Manchester is (I say to myself) a nice rest, a chance to catch up on your reading, have a glass or two, a meal, a little nap. But when you have done this kind of thing for months on end, your idea of a nice rest is to sit on your bottom at home, and limit your exercise to walking the dog.

I speak for myself, and I do know some cricketers, players and even reporters, who are so fanatical about the game that they never seriously seem to wish to do anything but play or watch it: but they are few. The man who never finds cricket boring is probably a cricket bore. An admirer of Disraeli once asked a favour of the great man: that he might bring his son to see him – and 'Would you give him one word of counsel which may stand him in stead all his life?' Disraeli groaned, at least inwardly, but consented, and offered this advice: 'My dear young friend, your good papa has asked me to give you a word of counsel. Here it is: Never ask who wrote the "Letters of Junius", or on which side of Whitehall Charles I was beheaded; for if you do you will be considered a bore, and that is something too terrible, for you, at your tender age, to understand.' (I give this story, which has variations, as recounted by G. W. E. Russell, *Portraits of the Seventies*, T. Fisher Unwin, 1916.)

There is much force in Disraeli's comment about bores, though I doubt if he experienced the acutely painful cricketing variety.

They are an affliction for a writer. They are no doubt good husbands and fathers, as Bernard Darwin said of men who missed short putts; they will almost always stand you a pint, but the price is high. For some years John Arlott, Henry Blofeld and I spent time choosing an eleven of English cricket bores, to play against an eleven of Australian cricket bores, for whom Jack Fingleton undertook the responsibility. How the contest would be decided we were never quite sure, for though there were plenty of candidates, we could hardly expect to command a satellite for a fortnight, which would have been necessary for an informed judgment. The mark of the true bore, what you might call the recognisably high-class cover drive, is the firm grip on the lapel, and the words 'You don't remember me, do you?' You can try a bouncer, saying 'No', but that produces the response, as he shrugs it off, 'I thought not. Well, I can tell you it was at . . .'

Some of them rely less on the cover drive than the gentle forward defensive stroke. Henry met one of the masters of this approach one day years ago at Northampton. This chap sat by his side for a long while, as if not observing the scribbles on the notepad, before saying, very quietly

'Press, I see.'

Henry, lured into the impression that this was no more than a polite neighbour, a middle-order batsman just up from the second eleven whom he could get out whenever he liked, nodded and smiled in his best Etonian manner.

'Er – yes.'

'You'll excuse my interest, but who do you write for?'

'Er – the *Guardian*' (Henry always writes for at least three different newspapers under three different names, but it was the *Guardian*' on that occasion).

'Oh, that's very interesting. I always take it. Yes, I think a man should take his local paper. Why, I've been reading the *Kettering Guardian* ever since I came to live in the midlands. That was about the time it amalgamated with the *Echo* and *Advertiser*. I suppose you remember the old *Echo*?'

This, Henry correctly decided, was the time for a maiden over, a gentle 'Afraid not', and silence. But because like all cricket reporters he is a touch conceited, he could not resist saying, after letting one or two go outside the off stump, 'No, no, it's the *Guardian* I write for, the London *Guardian*, used to be the Manchester *Guardian*, you know.'

This was a rank half-volley. 'Ah, do you now? Well, well, I'd no idea I was sitting next to somebody so distinguished. Well now, would you say, looking at this afternoon's play – no, no, I mustn't ask you what you would say, that would be cheating, I shall have to buy the paper to find out, shan't I? – but I'll tell you what I would say . . .'

He was well set, and the bowling flagged. Henry very nearly missed his edition that night, when at last he detached himself. He arrived in the press box pale and wan. 'Alan', he said to me, 'see that chap in the green jacket at the end of the row in front of the pavilion? You ought to go down and give him a net.' So I did, and very nearly missed my edition too. Mr G. Jacket was thenceforth a regular member of our side.

Our captain and number four batsman was Mr G. Voice (all members, you understand, were amateurs). Anyone who knew the Bristol ground, especially the members' bar, in the 1960s and 70s, will remember the mighty Gravel Voice. He was the Hammond of bores. No cautious opening strokes for him. He would bang a pint, unsought, in front of you – four runs – sit down in somebody else's chair beside you – another four – and slap you heartily on the back. Twelve runs before you had realised he had come in. Even bores of high quality usually begin with a look at the pitch and the length. As, 'I'ld be interested to know what you thought about that last decision', followed with a pause just long enough to allow you to say 'Er', before confidently resuming with 'It was my own opinion that . . .'

But Gravel, every word hoarsely and remorselessly dragged from that deep throat, never gave you a glimpse of sneaking even an 'er'. 'I don't want to know what *you* thought about that', he would begin, 'I'm telling you'. Short of downright rudery, which counts under the laws of bores as unfair play, he had you for the day. I am sorry that we never had the chance to pit him against Australia.

Looking back on this company, I also remember one who was not when you got to know him all that much of a bore: indeed, a pleasant fellow. But I would always have chosen him as an opening batsman, because his technique was so good. 'You don't remember me', he would say, as I have said the classical opening, and proceed swiftly, 'Come now, try. Tuesday, Wednesday, Thursday, Friday, Saturday, Sunday – ?' and you would reply, knowing what was coming, but helpless, 'Monday?'

'That's right', he would cry, a gale of laughter sweeping through him, 'Monday. Ted Monday. What'll you have?' Once he had got his joke over, all was well, but you knew you would have to go through it again, next time you saw him. Ted was a Hampshire man. I rather think, though I have forgotten the details, that Hampshire were well represented in our eleven, possibly because John Arlott was a magnet for bores, or possibly because he had a nose for spotting them.

The county of which I continued to see most, in those years after the war when I was only an occasional commentator, was Somerset. I remember the 1956 match against Gloucestershire. Gloucestershire won by a wicket in what would have been in any case the last over, a scrambled single by Sam Cook, a revenge for 1939. I had finished the normal periods of running commentary, but thanks to a helpful engineer recorded (on those great big twelve-inch discs, which took about thirty seconds to change over) the finish. We were proud of ourselves when it was broadcast – or a small part of it – later in the evening. If the game had gone on for another thirty seconds, we would have been out of disc, and changing over. This was not an uncommon experience at that time. I went to Exeter to record St Luke's College scoring a thousand points in a season (which had never been done before). They were playing Devonport Services, a good side at that time, and in no mood to give it away. St Luke's had reached 997 and were attacking: the critical question was 'Should we change discs?', but they might score at any moment. I hung on, gabbling away, and finally Gareth Griffiths went over, and the thousand was up. I made my way back to the recording car, and asked the engineer, a laconic man, whether we had managed it. 'Yes', he said, 'but one more stride and he'd have been running on the bloody label.'

I remember that 1956 match at Taunton not only for Sam Cook's winning hit, but the enormous, though vain efforts of Colin McCool. McCool scored over 150 runs in the match, without much support, and bowled finely in the last couple of hours. Mortimore was batting strongly for Gloucestershire and looking as if he might run away with the match. As McCool walked back – only a yard or two – he made a quiet, almost imperceptible gesture to Hilton at deep mid-on. Hilton unobtrusively dropped several yards deeper and straighter. Mortimore hit the next ball very hard but straight to him: he reached high and made the catch.

That was characteristic of McCool. He thought about the game a lot. Many Australian cricketers do, more than English cricketers probably, but McCool was in some ways an untypical Australian. He had a diffidence and gentleness, which do not always spring to mind as familiar Australian qualities: but he had plenty of Australian determination. Earlier that same season, Somerset had followed on against Gloucestershire at Bristol. It was only Monday afternoon, and clearly they were beaten to the wide. McCool went in at number three and scored sixty-odd, again unsupported, playing Cook and Wells admirably on a turning wicket. I said to him what a good innings it had been, and he accepted the compliment sombrely. 'Yeh, yeh, but we're losing matches, and I don't like losing matches.' A little later another Somerset player was out after a careless feeble stroke: as he came up the pavilion steps he beamed on us all and said, 'Not my day!' McCool was too polite to say anything, but I caught the look in his eye.

I came to know him well, and valued his friendship in the years he spent in the west. He came to Somerset relatively late in his cricketing life, and after he had made the decision to come, an extension of the qualifying period for overseas cricketers kept him waiting even longer. He had had a very successful season for Australia against Hammond's England team in 1946 to 1947. He played in all five Tests, scored 272 runs including a century at an average of 54; and took 18 wickets at an average of 27. In the second Test at Sydney he took 3 for 73 and 5 for 109. In the third at Melbourne he scored 147 for once out, and took three more wickets (he had scored 95 in the first Test, but hardly had a bowl because Miller and Toshack put England out twice on a ruined pitch). In the second innings of the last Test, when England only needed a good score to save something from the wreck of the rubber, McCool settled things with five for forty-four. Early in the tour, he had taken 7 for 106 against MCC for an Australian eleven at Melbourne. The MCC batsmen by all accounts played him fast-footed, traditionally *not* the way to play leg-spin. But since the batting order usually began with Hutton, Washbrook, Edrich, Compton and Hammond, it is also possible that he bowled pretty well. He took the wickets of eleven England batsmen: Edrich three times, Yardley three times, Hammond and Evans twice; Hutton, Compton, Fishlock, Washbrook, Ikin, Bedser and Wright once each. Only two of those wickets could be called tail-end ones, and he had Hutton, so masterly a player of leg-spin, leg-before when the great man had reached ninety-four.

In 1948, McCool was in England with Bradman's last team; but all summer he was hampered by a sore spinning finger, which would not heal. He did not play in the Tests, which distressed him greatly at the time, though he could be philosophical enough about it later. Australia had so many great cricketers at that time that McCool, in England, soon became only a vaguely remembered name. It did not arouse much interest in the west when it was announced that Somerset had asked him to qualify. Then it was realised, that because of the extension of the qualifying period, before he could play in the championship he would be 40 years old. Some rather contemptuous remarks were made about 'expensive old men'. So he was under some strain when he went in to play his first home championship innings against Essex at Taunton. He scored thirty-five when they were needed. I remember the large number of short singles which he took, no doubt to enliven the critical faculties of those who had spoken of 'old men'. He was always quick between the wickets. He was out trying to hook a straight ball from Bailey. The hook, he decided, was a stroke to used sparingly on English pitches, at least against Bailey (I recalled the incident to Trevor many years later, and he indignantly denied that it was only a straight ball – 'never bowled such a thing in my life'). McCool was constantly amending his technique that season, whenever he spotted a flaw in his method. Again and again he held the Somerset batting together. Nothing in his previous experience had equipped him for the task of holding up a losing side in a damp English summer. Only rain at the Torquay Festival prevented him from reaching two thousand runs. He took fifty wickets as well, but some of the old flexion had gone from the wrist, and it was rarely that Somerset scored enough runs to give a leg-spinner scope. At Taunton, against the 1956 Australians, he scored ninety and a hundred, and he would surely have strengthened the middle batting of Ian Johnson's touring side that year. After the second innings in that match, an old Somerset supporter declared it was the finest innings he had seen for Somerset at Taunton since the days of Palairet – and he had seen and admired Gimblett at his best. A few weeks later, after McCool had scored ninety against Gloucestershire at nearly a run a minute, the old man was not sure if he had not seen even a better.

This is the kind of tribute which will raise some eyebrows, and is often made in the warmth of the moment, but I mention it to give some indication of just how impressive McCool could be during his five seasons with Somerset. We hardly think of him as a stylist, and he was mostly a back-foot player, getting the greater number of his runs in the segments fanning out from point and square-leg. But he was enjoyable to watch, compact, tidy, combining powerful hitting with delicate placing. In the best Somerset tradition, he was always after the bowling, and in the best Australian tradition, he always relished a fight.

He did not quite come to terms with the West Country, as Sam Woods had done long before, and Bill Alley was to do later. His five years up, he went back to Australia. He missed the sunshine. 'There's no winter', he said, 'and the beer's better. And the F–––––off-spinners don't turn.' I think an additional reason was that he found some difficulty in accepting the conventions of English cricket, as it was then. There was a Somerset committee member, who liked and admired him, and would greet him with, 'Morning, McCool.' That committee member was seeking to be courteous. He would have thought it pompous to say 'Mr McCool', and impertinent to say 'Colin'. But it infuriated Colin. He thought it was a reflection on his status. He would have preferred something like 'Hi, Col, you old bastard.' The worlds were too far apart. But he had a son born in Somerset, who, with an impeccable qualification, came back to try his hand for the county in 1982. He did not win a place in the side. He was, like his father, a leg-spinner, and in that intervening generation, the leg-spinner had lost his place in county cricket. Indeed, the fact that his captain, Maurice Tremlett, decided to use Colin as a batsman rather than a bowler, had been an indication of the way things were going even in the 1950s.

Bill Alley joined McCool in the Somerset side in 1957. Few cricketers have had such a curious career. He never played for Australia. He was not chosen for the 1948 side, and came over here independently from New South Wales (for whom he had batted successfully) to go into the League. He was successful there as well. Not only did he make many runs, but he learnt to bowl as League professionals are expected to do. But it seemed likely, when he was 38 (and just conceivably a few years more, for he has always been vague about his age) that the Leagues would see him out. It was not as if he had a grand name to sell. The Torquay Festival were short of a man one year, and his name was suggested to the secretary, David Haines. 'Who did you say?', he enquired, sceptically. 'Well, he's supposed to hit the ball as hard as any man in the country.' 'Hum', said David, 'well, if he hits the ball as hard as any man in the country, I don't care whether he's called Bill Alley or Back Alley, he'll do.' I believe it was McCool who suggested his subsequent move to Somerset.

The announcement of Alley's impending arrival caused even less excitement in Midsomer Norton and Nether Stowey than had that of McCool himself. But the public soon began to warm to Bill. He was a left-handed batsman who did hit the ball very hard and very often. He bowled at medium pace, using the seam to move the ball from the pitch, just a little, either way. His high degree of accuracy proved valuable when the Gillette Cup arrived.

While McCool was in the side, Alley's degree of success for Somerset was only moderate. He did not seem so ready as McCool to adapt his batting technique to county demands. Repeatedly he would get out by sweeping at well pitched up balls on the middle, leg or even off stump. He would say, cheerfully, 'I know it gets me out, but it gets me runs as well.' He would also say, 'One of these days, when I get a bit of a luck from these F————— umps, I'll score 3000 in a season.' You could have got generous odds against this. Searching for a comparison, I suggested it would be a better bet to nominate Trevor Bailey (Walthamstow Avenue outside-right, retired) as Footballer of the Year.

In 1960 McCool went back to Australia. In 1961 Alley, left with the main batting burden, responded to the demand. He did score those 3000 runs. It was an astonishing autumn flowering. To score 3000 runs in a season is a feat which has only been achieved twenty times. Nobody has done it since Alley, and in the present pattern of first-class cricket, it is not likely to be done again. In all his first-class career, which lasted until 1968, he scored nearly 20,000 runs and took nearly 800 wickets. After some initial distaste for limited-over cricket, he became so good at it that three times he won match awards in the Gillette Cup. He became, in fact, that magic symbol of our times, a 'personality'. In 1973 *The Times* published a cricket supplement, and on its back page there were five brief essays about 'personalities of the game'. Those chosen were Illingworth, May, S. C. Griffith, Bert Lock and Alley. In such company did Bill find himself after that late and unexpected move to Somerset.

He was by then an umpire, and we wondered whether he would have the patience for it. He came in for some leg-pulling from his former associates. Brian Taylor was wicket-keeper and captain of Essex one day, and, by prearrangement, all the team moved smartly with him to their new positions, after only five balls had been bowled. Bill, after a puzzled glance at his counting pebbles, decided he had made a mistake and moved too. A few overs later, he permitted a seven-ball over. Not an Essex man had moved after the sixth was bowled. He took these little jokes in good part, and was too wily to be in trouble for long. He was soon on the Test match panel. He had, players have told me, an exceptionally high rate of accuracy in his decisions. Nor was he ever a man to be bullied, which has unfortunately become a necessary quality in a Test match umpire. The only criticism I have ever heard of him (leaving aside the inevitable curses of batsmen in thrawn moments) was that he was inclined to be too chatty at tense times in the middle. But conference maketh a ready man.

Bill settled happily in Somerset, with his infinitely delightful and forbearing Blackpool wife, Betty. He became one of the most popular men ever to have played for the county, though he was much more of what the English public thinks of as a 'typical Australian' than McCool. In my view, McCool was the better all-round cricketer, more consistent, tougher in a crisis. McCool did nothing to equal Alley's 3000 in a season, but Alley did nothing to equal McCool's 18 wickets in a series against England.

Of the other Somerset cricketers in those decades after the war, I had already seen Gimblett and Lee, Andrews and Hazell. Nor was Tremlett altogether new to me, for I had seen him play more than once during the war, for Taunton CC against the school. I recall a big six on to the railway line, and writing in the school magazine that if the Cornish Riviera had been passing, it would have been derailed. On his day he could be almost as fine an attacking batsman as Gimblett. It was maddeningly characteristic of Somerset cricket that though they both made heaps of runs, and frequently batted together, they never chose the same innings in which to appear at their best. That would have been an unforgettable day, a 450 for 2 day.

Maurice Tremlett first joined Somerset, however, as a prospective fast bowler. He had the build for it, and I often saw him bowl a ball as fast as anyone in England could in the late 1940s – not, given the time, the most blandiloquent of praise. In this capacity, he went on two tours for MCC, without doing very well, though he did get Walcott and Weekes out in Tests. He lost his bowling form suddenly and disastrously in the middle of a Somerset match, and never recaptured it. It is constantly said that cricket is a game played in the mind as much as the body, and this can no more be accepted as eternal truth than any other commonplace remark. Yet I can think of a number of instances when a fine cricketer has found himself in trouble, the mind unable to impose its command on the muscles, through a mental rather than a muscular failure. Tremlett suffered from this sometimes as did Gimblett.

E. W. Swanton once described Tremlett as a 'likeable but somewhat complacent cricketer'. This, I think, was a misjudgment of a sensitive man, whose large build and pink, confident face belied some inner tensions. He built up a second career as a batsman, scored two thousand runs in a season, and became Somerset's first professional captain. Perhaps E.W.S. was thinking of Tremlett's captaincy, a capacity in which he was certainly cautious, but professional captains needed to be cautious in those days. Yes I can see how the word 'complacent' crept in. There was an evening at Torquay in the middle 1950s, when after the Cricket Festival Ball, someone – I believe it was Maurice himself – suggested a midnight swim. When we got down to the beach, it did not seem quite such a good idea for a chilly morning towards the end of September, but we all mustered our courage and had a dash, except M. F. Tremlett. He changed into his bathing trunks, but was content to stand, looking even more than usually like Apollo, on the brink, loftily dipping a toe now and then. His wife Lee, on the other hand, swam out further than anybody, almost out of Torbay itself. Maurice, as a captain, would have been more successful with a dash of his wife's adventurous spirit.

Harold Stephenson succeeded Tremlett in the captaincy. I suppose you could not call him an outstanding captain either, but he was an exceptionally good wicket-keeper, who went on tour to Pakistan with England and must have been close to selection on several other occasions. He also had a very pretty wife, Connie. The Somerset standard of beauty in wives at that time was high. But I have ceased commenting on them, at least publicly, since I mentioned in a report that I had missed some vital incident or other because I had been talking to 'a pretty umpire's wife'. *Times* readers, never pleased by slipshod English, descended upon me ferociously, demanding to know who was the pretty umpire. I hope Mr and Mrs Kenneth Palmer have forgiven me by now.

I see I keep implying that Somerset players have been hard done by in selection, and this is a frequent provincial habit: 'no chance when you're playing for an unfashionable county'. But there was possibly some truth in it at one time, though I doubt if there was ever any deliberate prejudice. It was a matter of distance and frequency – remember I am thinking of a time before television and video recordings were so common. However hard the selectors tried to span the country, a player was likely to be seen more often on one of the central grounds, and thus had more opportunity to make an impression. Conceive a situation when a selector comes down to Taunton. He is immediately noticed. The buzz goes round. Who has he come to watch? Gimblett? Gimblett scores nought and one. The selector then returns to London and sees Edrich (W.J.) score nought and one. But he is much more likely to see Edrich again in the near future (or, if he is a northern selector, Washbrook): and a hundred comes up, and the failures are forgotten, and besides neither Edrich nor Washbrook were bothered by the presence of a selector – they are taken for granted at Lord's or Old Trafford. I have just invented this example, but I dare say something of the kind has happened from time to time. Selectors are aware of the problem, but they too are human and like to trust to the evidence of their eyes.

This leads me to another thought, and takes me back to Harold Stephenson. At one time it was widely said that he was a poor wicket-keeper 'after five o'clock in the evening' (that is, after a long day in the field). This was a *canard*: what had happened was that a single supporter, or (more likely) a single pressman, noticing that Stephenson had dropped a catch after tea, thought it would be a knowledgeable thing to say, and passed the word along with a solemn informed wag of the head. In no time at all, people who have not seen Stephenson keep wickets for months or years, are saying, 'Pity he's no good in the last hour'. Many cricketing reputations have been made or lost in such a way. There is rarely any deliberate animosity in the propagation of such yarns, and guiltily I feel that in my youth, anxious to make an impression, I propagated one or two myself. But when I heard this said about Stephenson, I did watch him carefully for his supposed fault, and the theory was rubbish.

There is one more Somerset cricketer of this time of whom I wish to say a few words: Johnny Lawrence. Johnny bowled leg-spin for Somerset from 1946 to 1955, and batted in the middle of the order (9000 runs, 800 wickets, and he did not begin until he was 32 years old). He was a Yorkshireman, but Yorkshire, even in those days, did not believe in wrist-spin. In 1950 he missed the 'double' by only nineteen runs. He was a smart catcher close to the wicket; he bowled a good googly. Tom Pearce, then the Essex captain, experienced some trouble spotting it. He ultimately decided to play right forward, down the line of the ball, to smother the googly and let the leg-break take care of itself. If he kept his wrists loose and, provided he was well forward, he reckoned the ball would not carry to the slips. He had some successes with this method. I recall Johnny telling me that he would reply by developing a faster ball. This seeemed improbable because he was one of the slowest bowlers I have ever seen. There were times when he would deliberately bowl slower and slower, until he almost reached the state of Sir James Barrie, who declared that he could bowl a ball so slow that if he did not like the look of it he could run after it and catch it. Whether the faster ball ever materialised, I doubt – certainly I never saw it – but accounts with Pearce and with most other batsmen he met were square by the end.

He was a little man. David Foot has written that 'he didn't seem much taller than the stumps'. But it is often an advantage for a leg-spinner to be on the small side. Colin Cowdrey, a marvellous bowler at Tonbridge, felt that he lost the gift because he grew too tall and could no longer throw them *up*. J. H. Cameron, who was at Taunton shortly before I went there myself, was another leg-spinner who had five years in the school eleven. He took all ten wickets in an innings for the Rest v. Lord's Schools, won a Blue at Cambridge, played for Somerset and was later Vice-captain of the West Indies. But according to A. G. Marshall, a wise judge of cricket who watched over his school career, he was never so good a bowler as in his first couple of years in the school team, the merest slip of a lad. Cameron did not become a tall man, but his wrists thickened, the venom went out of the spin. Johnny Lawrence kept the suppleness in his wrists to the end.

He was a jolly, kindly man, and perhaps the biggest contribution he made to Somerset cricket was his laughter and comradeship in the dressing room, at a time when things were generally going badly. He was a conscientious Methodist and refused to play on Sundays even for a fellow cricketer's benefit. He did not change his mind when it came to his own benefit year, though the Sunday games usually made more money for the fund than the 'benefit match' itself. He did not take money from raffles either. The benefit was still a fair success, partly because the Methodists rallied round.

I took part in a match on his behalf, on a Saturday after the end of the season, for a BBC eleven against Somerset on the Old Bristolians' ground at Failand. I still have the cyclostyled scorecard of that match, though without the scores, which is just as well. I will give myself the pleasure of reproducing the names of the teams.

SOMERSET	BBC XI
J. Lawrence (captain)	A. Gibson (captain)
M. F. Tremlett	J. P. W. Mallalieu
G. Lomax	P. Scott
J. Hilton	J. Watson
H. Stephenson	W. H. R. Andrews
L. Angell	J. A. Gregory
C. McCool	P. M. Beech
K. Biddulph	D. Wood
J. McHahon	D. Hawkins
H. Hazell	A. Symons
F. Norman	A. Ringer

The team list needs a little annotation. The BBC mustered a most impressive display of talent, but not very much of it was cricketing talent. It is true we had Bill Andrews, on the strength of his explosive summaries, but Somerset were not going to be bowled out by Bill, even in a light-hearted game, and he took nought for eighty-six. Jack Gregory, the England rugby international and athlete, batted and bowled well for us (it is a pity he has not done more broadcasting, because he has a talent for it). Patrick Beech, who later became controller of the midland region among other impressive jobs in the BBC hierarchy, was a capable wicket-keeper, though never (he has sometimes reminded me) quite the same man again. Otherwise we were good triers no more. Jack Watson enlivened us not only on the field, but off it, by his commentaries on the public address system. When Bill Mallalieu (later Sir William, Labour MP for Huddersfield East) went in to bat Jack informed us that as a matter of principle he was only allowed to hit towards the right. 'A. Ringer' represented Dr K. C. P. Smith. He is a bulky man, and had been made up by the Bristol Old Vic as W. G. Grace, beard, red-and-yellow cap, cocked toe and all. The resemblance to the old pictures was startling, until he actually batted.

Somerset scored hundreds and hundreds, and cleverly delayed getting us out until the very last over. Indeed at one time it looked as if the match must be drawn. It was agreed that every man on our side must at least break his duck, and this proved tricky in the case of Peter Scott, whose vast and varied abilities stopped short of cricket. Despite the best efforts of the bowlers, he simply could not make contact with the ball, and there was only a minute or two to go, one wicket to fall. A plan was secretly evolved (I was batting at the other end). Tremlett bowled a fast, widish one, Stephenson let it go for four, and the umpire, Andy Wilson, omitted to signal the byes. A boundary for Scott! He said afterwards, 'Do you know, I don't really think I touched it.' But he said it with a twinkle. We had not fooled him.

I think this must have been the only cricket match to be reported both by the *Methodist Recorder* and *Tribune*.

VII

The Vly Be on the Turmut

I be a turmet hower,
Vram Gloucestershire I came;
My parents be hard-working folk
Giles Wapshaw be my name.
   The vly, the vly,
   The vly be on the turmut,
   An' it be aal me eye, and no use to try
   To keep um off the turmut.
Eighteenth-century Gloucestershire song

Somerset and Gloucestershire matches, however the counties may be doing in the championship, have a tang of their own. Cardus has told us how once on a bank holiday he forsook his familiar Lancashire and Yorkshire, and came west to watch Somerset and Gloucestershire, thinking he would have a bit of fun for a change. He found a slow, grinding match, which might have been going on at Old Trafford or Bramall Lane. He should not really have been surprised. Somerset and Gloucestershire matches can be dashing and gallant (as Yorkshire and Lancashire matches can be) but there is a lot at stake, and neither side likes losing.

Somerset was granted first-class status in 1891, and beat Gloucestershire twice that season by ten wickets at Taunton and by an innings at Cheltenham. Gloucestershire had already won three championships more or less. The championship is usually held to have begun in 1873, in which year they were joint top with Nottinghamshire. In 1876 they were undisputedly top and again in 1877. In 1880 they were joint champions with Nottinghamshire again. But the championship was a haphazard affair in those days, run by the press so far as it was run by anybody. There was no agreed method of deciding who won, or even who was qualified to play, until MCC took the matter in hand in 1895.

Since those early days, Gloucestershire have had on the whole the better of their matches with Somerset, though they have never again won the championship. Nor have Somerset, as I write, ever won it, though in recent years they have won all three one-day competitions. There have been two occasions when Gloucestershire should have been champions.

In 1930, when they had one of their strongest sides – with a fast bowler it would have been their strongest ever – they were beaten by the system. Under any other method of scoring points for the championship they would have won. Lancashire were first, winning ten matches out of twenty-eight, losing none. All sides at this time played twenty-eight matches. Gloucestershire were second, winning fifteen, losing four. Yorkshire were third, winning eleven and losing two. Nottinghamshire were fourth, winning nine and losing one. Kent were fifth, winning twelve and losing seven. The reason for these absurd positions was the way first innings points were awarded: a win earned eight points, a lead on the first innings in a drawn match five. Even if you were behind on the first innings in a drawn match, you got three. You could win the championship on first innings points, and Lancashire did that year. Next year they had changed the system, so ridiculous had it become, but that was too late for Gloucestershire. They played well again in 1931, and came second, but a long way behind Yorkshire, who were laying the foundations of their great side of the 1930s. It was the first full season of Verity and Bowes.

The captain of Gloucestershire in 1930 was B. H. Lyon. I must pause here, because in later years I came to know him a bit, through his occasional visits to Oxford (he had been at Queen's, my own college) and his associations with Radiodiffusion. I saw very little of him on the field of play, but he was a good cricketer, an attacking batsman, a brave fieldsman close to the wicket. His principal fame, however, was won as a county captain.

Beverley Lyon went to school at Rugby, where he headed the averages, and was chosen for Lord's Schools in 1918. He was nearly four years younger than his brother, M.D. (usually known as Dan) who had preceded him at Rugby. Dan was possibly the better batsman, and had the additional advantage of being able to keep wicket. Indeed, he was unlucky not to be chosen as second wicket-keeper for the 1924 to 1925 tour of Australia. Neither of the Lyons played for England though both were picked for the Gentlemen. It is said that they tossed up as to which should go to Oxford and which to Cambridge, and also which should play for Gloucestershire and which for Somerset. This did not indicate a lack of fraternity. It was just that they felt it would be unfair to the opposition to have two Lyons on the same side. Dan went to Cambridge and Somerset. It was a fortunate toss for Gloucester-shire, simply because as things turned out Beverley was able to give more time to the game.

He won his Blue for Oxford in his second year, and made a pair, to the pleasure of his brother, who was keeping wicket for Cambridge. In 1922 he did better, scoring fourteen after setting out as if he intended to score a hundred in an hour (the witness for this is Robertson-Glasgow, who was playing in the same match). It did not matter, for Cambridge were beaten by an innings and 227. He first played for Gloucestershire in 1921, and did well in occasional appearances over the next few years. For the 1929 season they invited him to be captain. He decided to put his business cares apart for just a few seasons and enjoy himself.

His best stroke as a captain was achieved before he had even taken office. In the nets at Lord's he happened to bat against a ground staff bowler, called Goddard. Goddard had tried to bowl fast for Gloucestershire for six years, but had not done very well. His contract was not renewed, and he was grateful to have a job as a net bowler. However, as most MCC members did not take much bowling out, and did not much enjoy it when they were, he decided to bowl off-spin from a comfortable short run. Lyon spotted him at once and carried him back to Gloucestershire, thus creating the spin partnership of Parker and Goddard which so nearly took them to the championship. While Lyon was captain they did not always do so well, but they finished most of their matches. In 1934, for instance, they won twelve matches, only one less than the champions, Lancashire – but they lost ten. Lyon was as keen on a proper result as Stuart Surridge a generation later, or Sam Woods a generation before. It was Sam who had, I believe, coined the phrase that draws were only any use for swimming in. It was Lyon who invented the 'freak' declaration as it was called. In 1931 at Bramall Lane there had been no play for two days, and Lyon realised that if both sides declared their first innings closed at once, they could still play on the third day for full points, by then fifteen. Greenwood, the Yorkshire captain, agreed. After four formal byes had been bowled by each side (I am not quite sure why this was thought necessary, unless it was to awake the public as to what was going on) they went at it all day, before an increasing, and increasingly delighted crowd: delighted, that is, except that Yorkshire lost. I remember it well. I was infuriated, far away. I felt that Yorkshire had chucked it away. I cannot have been the only Yorkshire boy or man to feel like this.

Lyon suggested first-class cricket on Sundays and a knock-out competition, and lived to see both taking place before his death in 1969. I did not much care for either innovation, any more than I did for his Radiodiffusion activities, but it shows the originality and breadth of the man's mind. He had no funeral. He bequeathed his body to the Royal College of Surgeons – still looking for a positive end to the match.

The next time Gloucestershire should have been champions was in 1977, a hundred years after their first, when they lost on the last afternoon a match against Hampshire they had seemed to be winning easily. But it would make too rough an intrusion even into a loose chronology to tell that story now. I return to their matches against Somerset. For lengthy periods it was rare for Somerset to win, although the games were not often one sided, and there was frequently some unexpected twist to the play. At Bristol, in particular, Somerset found it hard to win. After the first few years, Gloucestershire almost always staged the Somerset match at Bristol. Somerset usually played them at Taunton, though sometimes at Bath, if the bank holiday happened to coincide with Bath's cricket festival.

Perhaps the most memorable of all their matches was at Bristol in 1895. That year, W. G. Grace, almost 47 years old, scored a thousand runs in May, which had never been done before. Of those runs, 288 were scored in a single innings against Somerset. It was Grace's hundredth hundred: the first time *that* had been done. To realise the magnitude of the achievement, you must remember that at that time nobody else had scored so many as fifty. Grace batted for 320 minutes with 38 boundaries (all fours, of course). Champagne was brought on to the field when he reached his century with the aid of a full toss from Sam Woods, who was more nervous than the batsman lest he should accidentally get him out.

Forty years later, in this same Bristol encounter, Hammond scored his hundredth hundred. Four times in four years he scored a hundred against Somerset at Bristol. The Somerset bowlers must have felt weak at the knees as soon as they got off the train at Temple Meads, or more probably Ashley Down (not many cricketers ran to motors then), surrounded by Gloucestershire supporters come to watch the execution. G. L. Jessop was another terror to Somerset. In 1904, he scored sixty-one in twenty-four minutes, forty-five of them from fourteen consecutive balls. In 1905, he scored 234 in just over two and a half hours, which was not regarded as one of his faster innings.

In 1914, on the weekend war broke out, Gloucestershire won by a wicket. They needed seventy-seven in the fourth innings and lost their first five for ten. In 1920, J. C. White bowled Gloucestershire out, nearly on his own, for twenty-two, but Somerset still lost by four wickets. In 1921, Parker took all ten in an innings, and Gloucestershire won by one wicket. This was a characteristic pattern for the time: a good match but Somerset just losing. In 1934, they managed to win at Bristol by thirty-nine runs (eleven wickets for White), but that was only their third win at Bristol since the First World War, and it was 1960 before their next. Indeed, from 1949 to 1960 Somerset did not beat Gloucestershire anywhere.

Many of the matches since the Second World War I have been able to see myself. Graveney and Milton were heavy scorers against Somerset, though they usually took their time about it especially at Bristol. The Bristol pitch was then said by batsmen to be very slow and low, making stroke-making impossible. 'Doesn't give you a chance of a cover-drive', it was explained to me by their wicket-keeper, Peter Rochford, who had once been invited by George Emmett to open the innings (only once) and ever afterwards held ambitious notions of his batting. Sam Cook, who I think was never asked to open the innings, heartily concurred. Even he could not find the pace in the pitch to make his cover-drive, or possibly his late cut.

I remember this conversation well, over the fourth or fifth pint at *The County Ground Hotel* in Nevil Road, But even then, a young man overawed by county cricketers, pleased to be on drinking terms with them, I felt that it was too simple an explanation for so much boring play. That there was something in it, I have, looking back, no doubt. Certainly Tom Graveney did something to prove the point after his move to Worcester, but many other factors were involved in that sea-change.

Sam Cook was a good slow left-arm bowler. He played for England only once in the first Test against South Africa in 1947. It was a plumb Trent Bridge wicket, and Sam took nought for 127 in 30 overs. Most county cricketers at the time – admittedly those to whom I talked were likely to have west country affiliations – thought him a better bowler than Howorth of Worcestershire and Young of Middlesex, who played in thirteen Tests between them without much success from 1947 to 1949. But life was hard for English left-armers then, and I dare say that Sam was quite relieved to be out of the way of the Australian thunder and lightning in 1948. I have often thought that Verity, had he not been killed in action in 1943, would have been by far our best spinner in those years. He was born in 1905, two years after Hammond and three before Bradman. These were the captains in the first postwar series. Verity was the kind of bowler who lasts for a long time and had a good record against Bradman.

Sam was, and remains – now an umpire – an equable, unhurried man. He was a plumber from Tetbury, a market town in the Cotswolds, a beautiful town with a magnificent church, and lots of other handsome old buildings. It must have been a good town in which to be a plumber: no shortage of work. Sam (his name was Cecil, and I have never understood why he was called Sam) arrived at the Bristol ground one morning in the spring of 1946, when the Gloucestershire players were warming up. Nobody was expecting him. He introduced himself to the captain by saying, 'I'm Cook, from Tetbury'. He was given a net, and was signed on by lunchtime. I say he came 'from Tetbury', but this is not quite accurate. One Saturday evening, from the Grand Hotel in Bristol, I volunteered to drive Sam home to Tetbury. It was not anywhere near the route I had proposed to travel, but I was still dazed by mingling with first-class cricketers. As soon as we got into the car Sam fell asleep. I drove him to Tetbury. When we arrived at the market cross, I woke him up and enquired, 'Which way now?' He rubbed his eyes, and said, 'Come too far. About five miles back.' So I retraced the five miles, with possibly the thought in my mind that first-class cricketers were not all they were cracked up to be.

What is much more astonishing than Sam's solitary Test is that Tom Goddard should only have played eight times for England and only once against Australia. Gloucestershire spinners in those days did not seem to have much luck with the England selectors. Dennett, whose career lasted from 1903 to 1926, a slow left-hander, took more than two thousand wickets at an average of less than twenty, but was never capped. He had Rhodes and Blythe to contend with, which is a sufficient explanation. Parker, who started in 1903 and went on until 1935, played for England only once in 1921, when he took two for thirty-two against Australia in the one innings the Australians had. On several other occasions he was summoned to the ground, and left out from the final selection. The most notable of these was in 1926 at Headingley, when the England captain, A. W. Carr, after leaving him out, put Australia in, and Macartney scored a hundred before lunch. Parker took 3278 wickets in his career (only Rhodes and Freeman have taken more), and his average, like Dennett's, was under twenty.

The omission of Parker from England sides can be explained on the grounds that he was a difficult customer (which was true, but many difficult customers have played successfully for England, and perhaps even more for Australia) and that he lost his magic on dry pitches (which cannot have been true: as if he could have taken all those wickets on damp ones!). In 1930, when he was 47 years old, an aeroplane was chartered to fly him to Leeds, but, as he said, 'They signalled that the pitch was dry and I flew away again.'

Tom Goddard took fewer wickets than Parker, a mere 2979, and at a higher average (19.84 against Parker's 19.46). He would much have liked those last twenty-one wickets to put him into the 3000s. As it is, including the wickets he took when he was a fast bowler, before Beverley Lyon rescued him from the Lord's nets, he is only fifth in the bowlers for aggregate of wickets taken (J. T. Hearne, who retired the year after Goddard began, holds fourth place). Goddard's Australian Test came at Old Trafford in 1930 when he took two for forty-nine in Australia's only innings. Then he played twice against New Zealand in 1937; three times against South Africa on tour in 1938–9; and twice against the West Indies in 1939. In those eight Tests he took twenty-two wickets at an average of twenty-six, figures respectable enough in a run-soaked decade.

It is one of my pleasures that I came to know Tom quite well, though chiefly in his retirement. He was a tall man with a craggy, genial face, and vast hands which never looked better than when clasping a pint: the horny hands of toil. His own explanation of why he was chosen for England so rarely was, 'Well, I were a good bowler, but I weren't quite so good as Hedley, and they only picked me when they left Hedley out'; and he would go on to say how often he and Hedley – whom he much admired – had often discussed this, and how Hedley would say, 'They should pick us together, Tom, then we'd have 'em going different ways.' Verity, you will remember, was a slow left-hander whose natural turn was from the leg. Tom's theory was not quite accurate – they did play together three times in South Africa – but in his Tests in England Verity was left out. In one of those South African Tests Tom did the hat-trick, which became particularly famous because a youthful E. W. Swanton happened to be broadcasting at the time, direct line to the BBC, then unusual. Hat-tricks are a fortuitous standard of bowling merit, and there has never been a legal definition of what constitutes one. Some unexpected bowlers have taken them at one time and another – who now remembers the Derbyshire demon, E. J. Gothard? But only seven bowlers are recorded as taking them in Test matches for England, and Tom was proud of his.

He was only 65 when he died, which seemed no age at all for such a vigorous man. The last time I saw him was when he came into the studio at Bristol to share in a discussion on the diminishing role of the spinner in cricket. Various theories were put forward. He gave them all a courteous hearing. In his heart he believed that the modern spinners were not good enough. I have even heard him criticise Laker; mild criticism to be sure, but in the 1960s it was like speaking disrespectfully of the equator. Nor was he a profound critic of batsmen: they existed only to be got out – with some reservations about Walter Hammond, with whom he shared digs for many years, and against whom he never had to bowl except in the nets.

Tom was sometimes mastered but would never admit it to himself. There were many occasions when the end of a long, hot day, the batting side 400 for 4, would still find him optimistically, unweariedly, spinning them up. But the 1948 Australians gave him a terrible hammering at Bristol, and he had to retire with a bruised hand. He later averred that he would have had them out but for the bruise, but it was hard to believe. Bradman, who was not playing in the match, has described (in *Farewell to Cricket*, 1953) how he had told his young off-spinner, Ian Johnson, to watch Goddard's methods closely, 'for here was a chance to get some education from a really great English bowler. Goddard', he goes on, 'probably couldn't remember when he had a worse match – Ian Johnson has seldom had a more successful one. You see, one has to take into account the quality of the opposing batsmen.' Morris scored a hundred before lunch and 290 on the first day. Ian Johnson did not think he had learned much. Tom suspected that the Australians had been deliberately instructed to 'hit him out of the firing line'. But it was not only Australians who thought that day that Tom's career was about to close. A line from Byron was quoted: 'Poor Tom's no more, and so no more of Tom.' Gloucestershire men, young and old, mourned his passing, but he kept proving them wrong for several more seasons.

I must say another few words about the famous tie against the Australians in 1930. The Australians were set 118 to win in the last innings. Here is their score.

A. Jackson, lbw b Goddard	25
S. J. McCabe, b Parker	34
V. J. Richardson, st Smith b Parker	3
D. G. Bradman, b Parker	14
A. F. Kippax, lbw b Parker	0
W. H. Ponsford, run out	0
E. A'Beckett, c Lyon b Parker	2
C. V. Grimmett, c Seabrook b Parker	12
A. Hurwood, lbw b Parker	14
P. M. Hornibrook, lbw b Goddard	4
C. W. Walker, not out	0
Extras: 2b, 7lb	9
	117

Bowling:	O.	M.	R.	W.
Parker	35	14	54	7
Goddard	34.1	10	54	2

The Australians went to Bristol the day after they had won the Ashes at the Oval. They were unbeaten except for the first Test. After that defeat, they had been much too good for England, and would probably have won four to one had the matches been played out. It was Bradman's greatest season, and Grimmett's. They had asked for, and been granted, a postponement of the start at Bristol until two o'clock. Rain caused a further postponement, and play did not start until a quarter past four. By the close of play, Gloucestershire had been put in and bowled out for seventy-two.

Australia led by eighty-five on the first innings. It was a turning pitch, and that lead seemed decisive. Then Hammond, who had been no more than adequate as an England batsman that summer, scored eighty-nine, an innings which he reckoned among the best half dozen of his life. When Australia went in before lunch on the third day with that 118 needed, Lyon opened the bowling with Parker and Goddard. It did not seem a profitable move. At fifty-nine for nought, Australia were winning peacefully.

The collapse was sudden and dramatic. Australians who had gone into town to have hair cuts, or for some other amusement, had to be recalled by taxi. Yet the odds must always have been slightly on Australia. They needed only three to win with two wickets left. Then Grimmett was out, and Walker came in to join Hornibrook. Walker's face, according to Reg Sinfield, who was fielding in the deep, was green; and I dare say Reg did nothing to improve his complexion by cheerfully saying, 'What an awful time to come in! I've been in this position myself.' A leg-bye and a single to Hornibrook made the scores level. Thirteen more balls were bowled with no score. Then Goddard had Hornibrook leg-before with what is reputed to have been the loudest appeal he ever made (the second loudest in the previous over had been turned down). In the match, Parker took 7 for 104, Goddard 10 for 126.

There are a great many people still alive and hearty in Bristol who saw this match, and to mention it in cricketing company still brings forth a stream of reminiscences, and of argument. I refer those who want more details to the account by Horace Hutt, then of the *Western Daily Press*, in *100 Years of Gloucestershire Cricket*, where there is also a copy of the scoresheet of the last innings. 'The greatest match ever played on the Bristol ground', is usually the way the argument ends. But I have heard even older Bristolians state the case for the Yorkshire match of 1906, and though it was long before my time, I cannot resist reminding you of it.

Yorkshire had been champions in 1905, and if they won at Bristol were almost certain to be champions again. The Gloucestershire first innings of 164 was not thought to be a good performance, but was sufficient to give them a first innings lead of five, thanks to Dennett who took eight for eighty-six. In their second innings Gloucestershire scored 228, so Yorkshire needed 234 to win. The Bristol ground was full on Saturday 25 August. Matches then ended on a Saturday, often, if they ended early, a terrible waste of a Saturday afternoon gate; but the players had to travel over the weekend. There were few even among the posh amateurs who possessed cars and the Sunday railway service was not so good. At the day's beginning Yorkshire were twenty-eight for two, Tunnicliffe and Denton out. There was a stand by Rhodes and Taylor, then a collapse: Yorkshire 119 for 5; another stand by Ernest Smith and Rudston: 185 for 5, Yorkshire winning.

Jessop, the Gloucestershire captain, was bowling. He was not the bowler he had once been, still fast for an over or two, but erratic. Rudston, full of confidence went to cut him, and chopped down his wicket in making the stroke. Three more wickets fell quickly, one left with eleven to win. Ringrose joined Myers. Myers scored nine of them, and then Jessop, who had taken himself off, went on again.

I have spoken, years ago, to three careful cricket watchers who saw this match, and they were independently unanimous in saying that the Gloucestershire supporters were displeased at Jessop's decision. Although he was much admired, Jessop was not always a popular captain – he had a touch of arrogance. He had been bowling rather wildly, and Yorkshire needed only two runs. Sure enough, his first ball nearly went for byes down the leg side, but Board, the wicket-keeper, flung himself across and just managed to stop it. Two balls later, Ringrose was leg-before-wicket. Yorkshire had lost the match by a run. They went on to win their last match, but Kent with a game in hand overtook them. Thus it is always said by Yorkshiremen that this was the year they lost the championship by a run, though it is not strictly true.

At the Bristol ground there is still a frame of faded old pictures, headed 'The Great Cricket Match'. The big crowd stood in front of the pavilion cheering the winners, every one of them wearing or waving a hat. One of the curious things about the Edwardians, it strikes me, was their belief that anyone without a hat was indecently dressed: hence the expression 'hats went in the air' had a force quite unknown to us today (though that does not stop us from using it). Inside the pavilion, George Hirst, who scored 2000 runs and took 200 wickets that season (imagine it! and his county still not champions) shook Mr Jessop – as he would always have addressed him – warmly by the hand. Wilfred Rhodes, I dare say, scratched his head.

It is absurd to leave Gloucestershire without saying anything more about Hammond, who dominated the scene for so long. My difficulty is that I have written about him in print several times before. But, working on the old Greek principle, that a man may once say a thing as he would have it said but cannot say it twice, I reproduce an article I wrote about Hammond in a small book almost a pamphlet, edited by David Foot, published in – no, it is undated, but it was a few years ago. In the view of its authors (Derek Robinson was the third) it remains as fresh and sparkling as the morning dew, and you may still be lucky enough to obtain a copy if you write to the editor at 20 Downs Cote View, Westbury-on-Trym, Bristol. It has, of course, by now acquired a rarity value. David can even manage to keep the unsold copies under his bed; not one left, I understand, in the loft. It is called *Game for Anything*, which seems an appropriate comment on its rash authors. Anyway, this is what I wrote in one brief essay.

Soon after the death of Walter Hammond, talking to an old Gloucestershire friend, I was moved to quote Hardy's words – at the end of 'Tess' – 'The President of the Immortals had ended his sport.' My friend was familiar enough with Hardy's bitter Aeschylean reference, but would not have it. 'Why', he said, 'Wally was just about the President of the Immortals himself!'

Nevertheless it could be argued that Hammond's career, for all its grandeur, was pursued by an ironic fate, from its beginning to its end. He first played for Gloucestershire in 1920. He had no sooner begun than Lord Harris, the antediluvian tyrant of Kent, successfully challenged his qualification. That meant no cricket for three years. However, when he did start, he soon showed his quality, and would surely have been England's No. 3 in the Tests against Australia in 1926 (this was a famous series when England won back the Ashes after three consecutive heavy defeats). But he fell ill, and could not play.

In 1928, he went to Australia, and seemed to have set all his disappointments behind him. He scored a record number of runs for a series: two double-centuries, and two centuries in the same match. England won the series by a street, and there seemed no doubt that Hammond would be the greatest batsman in the world for the next decade.

But in this same series, a youngster called Bradman appeared in the Australian side, and after an uncertain start played an innings which won Australia the last Test – their only victory. The next year Bradman came to England, and with a display of flawless batting which has never been equalled, broke Hammond's records for a Test series both in aggregate and average. Hammond himself had a relatively poor series with the bat, though according to the accounts he was England's best bowler.

There it was. For the rest of his career, Hammond was only the *second-best* batsman in the world, and he was not a man who was content to be second-best.

All his cricketing life thenceforth seems, in retrospect, to have been overshadowed by Bradman. In 1932–3, in Australia, Bradman was partially 'tamed', as it was genteelly put, by Larwood's leg-theory, but he still averaged slightly more than Hammond. In 1934, Hammond had his poorest Test series, never scoring 50, and Bradman won the rubber with a triple and double century. Next time in Australia, Hammond scored two hundred at Sydney, to give England a two-nil lead. But Bradman scored prodigiously again, and England lost, three-two. On the last morning of the critical fourth Test, England still had a chance, but Hammond was out quickly. 'Ee', said George Duckworth, 'you wouldn't get Don out in first over with Ashes at stake.' It was not enough for Hammond to do well. He had to do better than Bradman.

In 1938, Hammond was captain of England, and Bradman of Australia. Two Tests were drawn and the third abandoned without any play. In the fourth Test at Headingley, Hammond scored 76 in the first innings, Bradman 102. This was just about the difference between the totals of the two sides. In the second innings, Hammond was out for 0, and from then on Australia were winning. England squared the rubber at the Oval, but Australia kept the Ashes, and since it was widely felt that we were the stronger side, there was no great delight.

Then came the post-war tour of Australia. Was Hammond right to go? Did he believe that one last tilt could right the balance with his ancient enemy? He had had a magnificent, if limited, season in England in 1946, and in Australia he scored plenty of runs in the state matches. But again he failed in the Tests, while Bradman went remorselessly on. In the first Test, Bradman had scored 28 when he seemed so obviously caught by Ikin at second slip that the English side did not bother to appeal. Hammond, at first slip, sat down with a sigh of relief. But Bradman stayed where he was, and when an appeal was ultimately made, it was turned down. At the end of the over, Hammond said to Bradman, 'That's a bloody fine way to start a series.' Bradman scored 187. The captains were scarcely on speaking terms for the rest of the tour. Hammond returned home heavily defeated, and never played regularly again.

Do not think for a moment that in looking at Hammond's career in this light I am unaware of his merits. The splendour of his off-side play was unequalled. He was for some years the best all-rounder English cricket had had since Grace – and I do not forget Wilfred Rhodes. He was the best batsman we have had since 1918, except just possibly Hutton (I count Hobbs as pre-1914). Hammond gave to cricket, and cricket gave to Hammond, everything – except the things he wanted most.

I saw his last county match, in 1951. Gloucestershire were in trouble with injuries, and he was persuaded to come back – after an interval of several years – for the Whitsuntide game against Somerset. I shall never forget the reception, from one of the biggest crowds I have seen on the Bristol ground. They had been kept waiting a long time while Emmett and Milton scored 200 for the first wicket. They were no more than mildly appreciative of the stand: it was Hammond they had come to see. When he came, he batted for half an hour or so, scoring 7, all in singles. There was not one forcing stroke. In the evening we watched him fielding at slip, where he had been supreme. He stood there immobile, scarcely bending. We discovered afterwards that he had strained a muscle, and he took no further part in the match. We hoped we might see him play again, but we never did.

His life after that had its measure of disappointments and difficulties, but these are not matters on which I am entitled to enlarge. I met him in Bristol shortly before his death. The impression he gave was of a cheerful stoicism, of a man who had not found life easy but had come to terms with it. He was only 65 when he died.

This is why I spoke to my friend in terms of the President of the Immortals ending his sport.

I am not particularly proud of that essay as a piece of writing, and perhaps the public were wise to leave the copies of *Game for Anything* under David Foot's bed. But it still represents what I felt and feel about Hammond. Tom Goddard knew him as well as most, and shared rooms with him for a long time. He would often talk about Walter (he was more often called 'Walter' than 'Wally' by those who knew him) in the most glowing and affectionate terms, but always came back to the conclusion, with a meditative shake of the head, 'Ah, but he was a moody man. A moody man.' With

Anthony Smith and John Mason, I was responsible for a radio programme about Hammond after his death. We interviewed a great many cricketers, and it was a word that cropped up again and again: moody. Cardus wrote of him, in his memorial tribute in *Wisden*, 'his cricket was, I think, his only way of self-realisation'.

It would not be quite true to say, however, that cricket was his only interest. Ben Travers indicates another, in his delightful little book of cricketing reminiscences, *94 Not Out*. Travers happened to be in Australia during the 1928–9 tour, and watched the Sydney Test, in which Hammond scored 251. Travers, before setting out from England, had bought a powerful pair of field glasses. His seat gave him a good view of what he calls 'a show-case of Sydney's beauty queens'. He had become a friend of Hammond, who, he says:

> not out at the luncheon break, or taking the appointed forty minutes off from first slip, as the case might be, would arrive at my side soon after the start of the interval. He would say nothing; merely hold out his hand for the field-glasses. There he would sit, the field-glasses making a detailed tour of the Ladies' Enclosure, until a few minutes before play was due to start again, when he would hand me back my field-glasses, say 'thanks' and disappear. Laconic.

Eddie Paynter, a great Lancashire and England batsman, was asked, towards the end of his life, who was 'the greatest in his time'? Without hesitation, he replied, 'Wally'. He added by way of explanation, 'My, he could shag 'em.' He was not thinking entirely of the bowlers.

Hammond inevitably overshadowed the other Gloucestershire batsmen of his time, even Charles Barnett, who very nearly scored a century before lunch against Australia in 1938. I never had much luck with Barnett. I would read about a dashing innings he had played and eagerly look forward to watching him: but I cannot remember seeing him make many runs. Luck has a lot to do with judgment of cricketers. To take an opposite example, I am still inclined to think that Willy Watson of Yorkshire was one of the great batsmen of his time and generally underestimated. For every time I happened to see Watson, even in his later days with Leicestershire, he seemed to make runs.

Jack Crapp was Gloucestershire's first professional captain, and

George Emmett succeeded him. They were both splendid cricketers, and I was certainly lucky with them. Of Jack I shall write when I come to Cornish cricket, for though Cornwall was not, for most of his life, his home, he was born there and never forgot his origins. George Emmett was the more elegant batsman, but Jack, on balance, the more effective. George had really appalling luck with his Test career. He was chosen only once in the toughest possible circumstances. In the second Test of 1948 against Australia, Hutton did not bat well. I did not see the match, but even so faithful a Yorkshireman as J. M. Kilburn has written that in the second innings 'Len really did fall below his own standards.' It was thought that he ran away from the bouncers of Lindwall and Miller. The England selectors took the terrific decision to drop him. It may, looking back, have been a good decision: 'at any rate', Jim Swanton has written, 'I never saw Len flinch again.' But it was obviously only a temporary measure. The question was, who would open with Washbrook at Old Trafford in the third Test? The choice fell upon George Emmett. It was a cruel one. He was a good player of fast bowling, but had no experience of it at this level. What is more he needed to score at least 50, probably 100, to retain his place in the side, because, having dropped Hutton for one match, the selectors could hardly be expected to drop Washbrook for the next. He was on a hiding to nothing. Lindwall got him twice for ten and nought. Washbrook scored eleven and eighty-five not out. Washbrook was dropped twice at square-leg early in his second innings, and George would sometimes wonder what might have happened if one of those catches had been held. But his moment had passed and he never played for England again. He was a small, neat man – 'dapper' was the journalists' favourite word – quick on his feet in defence, though in later years he was handicapped in his forward play because of a bad knee. His cut was a sight to see, and even if he was caught in slips or gully more often than he would have wished, he had the same excuse as Bill Alley for his pull – it got him a lot of runs. George was a firm disciplinarian when captain and on the whole a reserved man, but very good company when you came to know him. He had a gnomic grin and a dry wit. I went to interview him for the memorial programme for Hammond, which I have mentioned. His view of Hammond (which we did not record) was that 'he was the best of my time, though of course a bastard'. What we did record was his remark: 'Whatever else you may say about Walter, he could count perfectly up to six.'

This was a reference to Hammond's known habit of keeping the bowling when he was in form and the pitch was easy. Sinfield used to say much the same thing. One day he noticed that he had been in for three-quarters of an hour and had only scored three (or some comparable figure). He spoke to the umpire, an old friend, I think Bill Reeves. 'Bill', he said, 'I'd better be getting a move on. Never batted so slowly in my life.'

'Reg', said Bill, 'I've been counting. You've had seven balls so far.'

Hammond was at the other end. This is not necessarily a fault of Hammond's. It was no doubt in the interests of the side that he took nearly all the bowling. But it did become, sometimes, a little depressing for his companions.

In retrospect, we think of Sinfield as an off-spinner, perhaps what we would now call a medium-paced 'off-cutter', though that term was not known then. The Gloucestershire spin bowlers went in pairs: Dennett and Parker; Parker and Goddard; Goddard and Sinfield; Goddard and Cook. More recently there have been Allen and Mortimore, more recently still David Graveney and Childs. But Sinfield, though he took more than 1100 wickets for Gloucestershire, had begun as a batsman, usually an opening batsman, and scored more than 1500 runs.

Reg was not Gloucestershire born – he arrived *via* Hertfordshire and the Lord's ground staff – though he came to be assimilated to the county in much the way that Arthur Wellard became assimilated to Somerset. He did not play after the second war, but became until retirement a happy and popular professional at Clifton College. He also had played for England – once. It was an occasion he looked back to with satisfaction, the first Test of 1938. He scored only six runs in his only innings; and took only two wickets in sixty-three overs. The second was at the fag-end of a drawn match. The first was Bradman's, when the mighty man had reached his fifty, and that was considered a lifetime's accomplishment for an England bowler in those days. I misremembered the occasion one day in conversation with some friends. I was telling them how Sinfield had had Bradman leg-before, and he chipped in, with as much of severity as ever I heard in his voice, and said, 'Caught at the wicket, *if* you please.' He was, when I knew him, a ruddy-faced, greying man, a smile always lurking in his solemnity. He did not seem to feel hard done by that he never played again for England. He had got Bradman out.

Dennett, Parker, Goddard, Cook and Sinfield took about 11,000 wickets between them, and won eleven England caps, three of them against Australia.

In Gloucestershire's centenary year, 1970, a book, or large pamphlet, was published to mark the occasion. It was hoped that it would make some money to aid Gloucestershire's financial position, then dire. The contributors naturally worked from sheer goodwill. I think journalists are sometimes too soft about this kind of thing. When a player asks you for five hundred words or so for his benefit brochure, and you know (well, nowadays it is quite possible) that he will be getting fifty thousand pounds or so from his benefit, and he does not offer you so much as a pint in return . . . But young journalists do it, eager for the publicity, or the prestige of calling the great man by his Christian name. I record in passing that of the numerous articles that I have written for benefit brochures, I have received one letter of acknowledgement and one bottle of whisky. These came from that splendid chap, one of my favourite cricketers, Robin Jackman, the Shoreditch Sparrow.

However, this is a digression, and there is no doubt that Gloucestershire were very hard up in 1970 (if you take the trouble to go to Budleigh Salterton, I think you will find the remaining copies of the book, *100 Years of Gloucestershire Cricket*, stacked under Grahame Parker's bed). So I accepted the honour of writing a piece for it, and the difficult task of choosing 'The Best Gloucestershire XI'. This is the kind of project which, to be of any value, requires some preliminary qualifications. First, you have to decide approximately at which period of a man's life you are picking him. If, for instance, you were picking a world eleven, and considering Rhodes, would you consider him as the beautiful young left-arm spinner of 1899, or the England opening batsman of 1912, or the bit-of-both knowledgeable veteran of 1926? Just to say 'Rhodes' is not enough: you would be choosing three men not one. Second, since this was a Gloucestershire eleven, do you pick the men on their form for the county, or their form in all cricket? For example, W.G. scored less than half his runs for Gloucester-shire, but was undoubtedly a Gloucestershire man. Who was the most successful Gloucestershire bowler in Test cricket? It would be difficult to deny the claim of J. J. Ferris, who in nine Tests took sixty-one wickets at under thirteen runs apiece. But he took most of them for Australia, and only played for Gloucestershire when he was past his best. What about Tom Graveney? Should he be judged only on his form before he left Gloucestershire, with some of his best cricket before him? What about Procter and Sadiq and Zaheer?

And what kind of match is envisaged? If you are playing a timeless Test on an Australian pitch in the 1920s, you take all the batsmen you can and don't worry too much about the bowling (as England did in 1928). But what if you are picking a side to play Glamorgan at Swansea in a wet summer, or Kent at Maidstone in a heat wave? It is impossible to make rules about such matters, but after all it is only a game about a game. I chose a side to represent Gloucestershire in a three-day match under championship conditions, and everyone had to have an association with the county which could be deemed 'substantial'. The pitch they prepared on the Elysian fields was to be what cricketers call 'a good cricket wicket': it is fast, the ball comes on to the bat, encouraging stroke play, but lively. It helps the quicker bowlers a little in the first hour, it takes spin on the third afternoon. Such wickets scarcely exist anywhere *else* than the Elysian fields, or the imagination of cricketers who believe they would do the double every year if only they had a chance of playing on them. However, like it or not, this was the team at which I arrived, with the dates at which I would have chosen them appended:

> W. G. Grace (captain) (1871)
> C. J. Barnett (1938)
> W. R. Hammond (1928)
> T. W. Graveney (1953)
> J. F. Crapp (1948)
> G. F. Grace (1880)
> G. L. Jessop (1900)
> M. J. Procter (1969)
> P. J. Rochford (1955)
> C. W. L. Parker (1926)
> T. W. Goddard (1930)
> Twelfth man: C. L. Townsend.

You must remember that I was choosing this side in 1970. I suppose, since then, Zaheer would have to come in (though he took some time to settle down in the county, and played a full season without getting his cap), and Fred Grace or Jack Crapp would have to go. It would be a close call between Sadiq and Barnett. Also, Procter, of whom we thought then in Gloucesteshire principally as a fast bowler, would have to move up the batting order. Otherwise it still looks a pretty good one.

Grace, Hammond and Jessop it seemed to me were certainties. In case you think that I am just making a genuflection to W. G. Grace, I remind you that in 1871 he scored 2739 runs, at an average *more than twice* that of any other player. This was at a time when he was one of the fastest men over a hundred yards in the country – no resemblance to the patriarchal figure we see in the few action photographs taken in his old age. Procter was shortly to become a certainty. Parker and Goddard had much competition among the spinners, but I cannot really think that Gloucestershire have had, to this day, a better pair. It was hard to exclude Dipper, who came from Tewkesbury, one of the loveliest of Gloucestershire country towns. Shakespeare says Tewkesbury was famous for its mustard balls, though it is not exactly clear what he meant by it. Dipper could be called a kind of mustard ball, a left-hander who liked to give the ball a tonk. He must have been quite like Broad of the recent Gloucestershire side. (How appropriate, both names.) Dipper scored more than 28,000 runs for Gloucestershire, more than anyone except Hammond. Most of them came on the leg side. No, he was not elegant, but as Tom Goddard used to say of batsmen to whom he was reluctant to concede the higher virtues, uncommon awkward. Dipper played for England (Oh familiar Gloucestershire refrain) only once, at Lord's in 1921. He scored eleven and forty, and only two English batsmen in the match scored more. So he was not exactly a failure but his fielding was held against him. He was a slow mover, like the Severn as it slips sluggishly by Tewkesbury. So I felt Charles Barnett ought to open the innings with W.G., with another reluctant glance in the direction of Arthur Milton.

There could not be much argument about Tom Graveney, even though he left the county in some acrimony after Pugh had replaced him as captain. This was a silly business, which did not show any of the participants in a favourable light. But Tom was a great batsman and always a friendly fellow. It would be absurd not to have him in your best Gloucestershire eleven. Fred Grace and Peter Rochford were more controversial choices. Fred Grace is admittedly a guess on what he might have become rather than what he did. He was the only member of all the cricketing Graces who might, had it not been for his early death, have approached the mastery of the champion himself. And he was by repute one of the best outfields ever to play the game (remember someone is needed in the deep to cover for Tom and Charlie). In the first home Test against Australia, he caught out the mighty hitter Bonnor on the boundary, and the batsmen had completed the second run before the ball came down to the fielder. This is something you are not often likely to see. G. F. Grace died, the family always said, through sleeping in damp sheets at an away match. Should he commit such an indiscretion again, we have an admirable twelfth man in C. L. Townsend. In fact the older generation would choose him anyway.

H. S. Altham wrote of Townsend, 'had he been able to play regularly for his county in the years when he had become an England batsman, it is possible that he and Gilbert Jessop together would have played almost as big a role in Gloucestershire cricket as did Ranji and Fry for Sussex'. This is high praise from one of the best of judges. Townsend was primarily chosen for England (twice, in 1899) as a left-handed batsman, but is remembered as much for his bowling – from the back of the hand, right-arm, with fierce spin. He could also bowl off-breaks. It was a pity that the googly had not been invented in his formative years, for he had the kind of subtle mind to exploit it. I knew him a little, towards the end of his long life (he was 82 when he died). He looked very much what he was, an aging solicitor, and not at all what he also was, an aging cricketer who could have been one of the great all-rounders of a golden age.

As for Rochford: wicket-keepers are hard to judge over the years because the figures mean so little. With Goddard and Parker bowling, we must have a good *stumper*. Board must have been a good stumping wicket-keeper. Andy Wilson was among the best in the country in my time. Peter Rochford's playing career ended early, which I am afraid was largely his own fault. He was wayward, and did not get on very well with George Emmett. The end came when he failed to turn up at all one day at Cheltenham, having taken French leave to visit his home in Halifax, and missed his train back. But I have never seen anyone with a more natural talent for the job, and therefore picked him at his brief best, hoping that W.G. would manage to keep him in order.

This game of 'best elevens' is easy to play, but easily becomes boring: an occupation for a glass or two after dinner, not a rainy day. I promise not to play it again in this book barring one last recollection. I was once, in a television programme called *Late Night Line-Up*, asked to join with Sir Learie Constantine (as he then was) and Harold Pinter, in choosing an all-time world eleven. This must have been in 1965 or thereabouts. A more improbable trio of selectors could hardly be imagined, but we were presumably brought together for conversational potential as much as cricketing knowledge. Whether the viewers enjoyed it I do not know, but we did. This was the result:

> J. B. Hobbs
> V. T. Trumper
> G. A. Headley
> D. G. Bradman
> W. G. Grace (captain)
> G. St A. Sobers
> L. N. Constantine
> H. Larwood
> W. A. Oldfield
> W. J. O'Reilly
> S. Barnes

Sir Learie dissented at his own inclusion, but it was not meant simply as a conversational compliment. If you are choosing the best eleven in the world, you ought to include the best fielder. He did, however, insist on Headley at number three. 'And we must also have Bradman at number four, because Bradman was the White Headley.' Harold Pinter felt that a batting place should have gone to Hutton. I wondered myself whether it might be a better idea to open with Hobbs and Sutcliffe, for there can hardly ever have been so reliable an opening pair, but I knew that if we left Trumper out, Jack Fingleton would never speak to me again, and that was too high a price to pay. Ranji? Much argument. Hammond? It occurred to me going home on the train afterwards that we had not mentioned his name. A sad note on which to leave Gloucestershire cricket.

VIII

Hambledon Country

'Then fill up your glass! He's the best that drinks most;
Here's the Hambledon Club! Who refuses the toast?
Let us join in the praise of the Bat and the Wicket,
And sing in full chorus the Patrons of Cricket.'

During the 1950s I began to be asked to travel further afield to broadcast about cricket, and sometimes to write about it, but still most of the cricket I saw was in the south and west, and after Somerset and Gloucestershire the side I knew best was Hampshire. Hampshire in those days meant, above all, Desmond Eagar. I met him first when he broadcast a talk, 'County Captain', from the Southampton studio. They were more spacious days in radio and he had fifteen minutes for it – today he would be lucky to get three, and half of that would be taken up by an interviewer cutting capers. I do not think the talk has ever been published, and probably the script has long gone: a pity, because it gave much insight to the problems of running a county side.

There were those who thought, just before the war, that Desmond would make an England player and possibly an England captain. He had a successful school career at Cheltenham, whom he captained for two years, won a Blue at Oxford and made a promising beginning with Gloucestershire. One of his early county matches was at Bournemouth in July, 1939. He had come into the side after a successful Oxford season, leading their averages. Gloucestershire were forty-five ahead on the first innings, but then lost quick wickets against Baring and Heath. Eventually they recovered, declared and won the match, and their top scorer was young Eagar, forty-eight out.

After the war Hampshire advertised for a secretary-captain. Eagar applied and got the job. For more than thirty years he was their guide, philosopher and friend, until his sad, sudden death in 1977. As it turned out, after the long break, he was never quite so good a cricketer as his early admirers had hoped, but he maintained a fair county standard – 12,000 runs at 22 – and always batted with style, and was an outstanding fieldsman close to the wicket. His figures do not show how many times he lost his wicket trying to push things along at number six or seven, nor how many times he scored his runs when the going was hardest. For instance, there was a match at Bristol in 1954. Hampshire, 140 for 5, were struggling; only Rogers could handle the bowlers with any confidence. Eagar then joined his number one, they put on 147, and the match was won by an innings.

There were several secretary-captains of that period, the twilight of the amateur age, whose secretarial duties were nominal. Not Desmond. No man ever worked harder for his county, and much of the work was of a routine kind, you would think boring even to such an effervescent spirit. He never wilted under any number of club dinner speeches. If a few more Hampshire memberships could be coaxed from his audience, he counted the long hours well spent (and they could be *very* long hours – far too many clubs confuse the annual dinner with the annual general meeting). He was a good speaker, a good broadcaster and a good writer. He was for many years hockey correspondent of *The Sunday Telegraph*, often reporting from some bleak expanse with no stand, nor even a seat, and the nearest telephone about three miles away. He had only taken on the job because it occurred to him it was a way in which Hampshire need pay him less money (they declined the suggestion). He spent much time on *The Hampshire Handbook* (which soon became the best in the country), on the history of Hampshire cricket and collecting and annotating its library and museum. He could have had a choice of several careers, but decided that cricket was the thing for him, and the rest would have to be peripheral. In a slightly different way his son Patrick made the same decision: discovering he had a gift for photography, he concentrated on cricket photography, in which he rapidly reached the top of his profession.

Desmond took Hampshire to third place in the championship, the highest they had then achieved. This was in 1955, and to celebrate the occasion the team was given a dinner at the House of Lords. In 1975, they also came third and the result was generally described as 'disappointing'. He relished this contrast, rightly seeing it as a reward for his labours.

As a captain, he could sometimes be criticised for negative tactics, but for the greater part of his captaincy Hampshire were dependent upon seam bowling. As we saw Shackleton and Cannings bowling endless inswingers to close-set leg fields, over after over after maiden over, there were times when we felt that a spinner – especially a leg-spinner – would have been more interesting to watch, and would probably amount to the same thing in the end. But where was the leg-spinner? I remember at one time there was a plan to import Eddie Leadbeater from Yorkshire, but nothing came of it. On the other hand, Desmond's strategy was usually sound. He had a fine sense of timing for a declaration.

The first Hampshire side to win the championship, in 1961, was captained by Colin Ingleby-Mackenzie. Desmond had spent years building up the side, but it is fair to say that Ingleby-Mackenzie, more of a dasher and a touch rasher, deserved to crown the edifice. What a pity, people said, that Desmond had retired before Hampshire won the championship, his heart's desire! He did not share this view.

Here let me interpose a short lesson in the difficult Christian virtue of humility. If you can create, say, the best symphony in the world, or paint the best picture in the world, or sing the best song in the world, or preach the best sermon in the world, or play the best innings in the world – if you can do any such thing: and know it to be the best, and rejoice because it is the best, *but rejoice no more and no less than if anyone else had done the same thing*, then ... ah, then! you are a humble man. And I do believe that Desmond rejoiced in Ingleby-Mackenzie's success as much as if it was his own.

I was present at his last match, at the end of the 1957 season. It was something of a *Boy's Own Paper* ending, for the match was Hampshire v. Gloucestershire at Bournemouth, where eighteen years earlier an undergraduate's forty-eight had swung the match. I suppose he would have picked no other side to finish against, and no better way of doing it – Shackleton and Cannings, the old firm, dead on a length, the infield packed, a resounding Hampshire win. It was a moving moment when he ran up the pavilion steps for the last time applauded by both teams. There were tears in his eyes, and not only in his.

He was one of the best of the old-style county captains. He did good by stealth, and would have blushed to find it fame. His professionals made jokes about him, but not behind his back. They were very fond of him, and he got the best out of them. And he could be tough at times, as Ingleby-Mackenzie discovered when, still young, he took an early evening shower, and was suddenly required to bat. So even did his beloved wife, Marjorie, discover, when they had a tiff one morning over the breakfast washing-up. He made her so cross that she threw a cup at him. 'What made her even crosser', he said later in the day, 'was that I caught it.'

If Eagar, aptly named, was the light of Hampshire cricket, Shackleton was its day-labourer, and there was something appropriate in his name too, fettered endlessly to the bowling crease. 'Skipper says we make one change a day. That's middle of afternoon when he switches me to 't other end and lets Vic swan around in 't field for half an hour.' When historians look back on the period, they may well see in Shackleton its symbol. There was a flowering of really fast bowlers in the 1950s, but Statham, Tyson and Trueman left few successors, at least in English cricket. Spin was regarded increasingly as a secondary art. The picture of a typical county day of that time (and, I am afraid, still) has been a succession of seamers churning them in, waiting for something to turn up, giving nothing away. There has been a vast company of them, and none more assiduous, accurate and successful than Shackleton.

This is not intended to be a disparagement of him. It is no disparagement of an infantryman to say that he cannot lead a tank charge, and though tanks win dramatic battles, infantry is still needed to win wars. Shackleton was the infantryman *par excellence*. If all the other bowlers of his type had possessed his qualities, few batsmen would have reached a thousand runs a season. He took 2857 wickets, average 18.65, from 1948 to 1969. The bowlers who have taken most wickets in their careers (up to 1984) are: Rhodes, Freeman, Parker, J. T. Hearne, Goddard, Grace, Kennedy, Shackleton, Lock and Titmus (still taking them now and then). Rhodes, who took more than 4000, and occupies, as Altham wrote, 'a solitary and splendid niche in the temple of fame', was a slow left-hander, as was Parker, and Lock. Freeman bowled slow leg-spin. Hearne bowled at medium-pace, his stock ball breaking from the off, growing slower as he grew older. Grace, as a bowler, was an allsort, from fast round-arm in his lusty youth to slow leg-breaks (at least, theoretically leg-breaks) in his cunning age. Goddard and Titmus were off-spinners. Of course, spinners last longer than fast bowlers, so there is no really fast bowler in the list. The nearest you get to a fast bowler is Shackleton – or even his fellow Hampshireman Kennedy, who I am told could be quick at times, though he relied more on spin than seam. Herbert Sutcliffe wrote of Kennedy (*For England and Yorkshire*, Edward Arnold, 1935) that:

> his accuracy was as extraordinary as his stamina. He never tired, or, at all events, he never appeared to tire. Even at the end of a long day under the sun, he would go on for a final spell and the batsman who knew him realized there would be nothing given away. The batsman who did not know him quickly learned that Kennedy had a wonderful command of length, and, what is more, that when Kennedy was playing cricket he fought to the very last ball.

This could well have been written of Shackleton. I remember once joining in a commentary session when John Arlott was at Southampton, I at Bristol or somewhere, others scattered around. John began with an unusual tone of excitement. 'Here's some surprising news from Southampton, a real shock. Shackleton's not bowling ... Don't take it too seriously, have heart attacks or anything. He's had to leave the field for a few minutes to change his boot.'

There is an interesting thing about that list of bowlers who have taken the most wickets. Consider their Test match appearances. Rhodes played in fifty-eight Tests, twenty-one against Australia, but there was a time when he was chosen as a batsman rather than a bowler. Grace played in twenty-two Tests all against Australia, but was never chosen for his bowling. Hearne played in only twelve tests all against Australia, in the span 1891–99. Freeman played in twelve Tests, only two against Australia. Goddard and Parker, as I have already mentioned, had nine Tests between them, one each against Australia. Kennedy played in five Tests against South Africa on the 1922–3 tour. 'It is one of the curiosities of cricket', says Sutcliffe, 'that he never went to Australia.' Kennedy took thirty-one wickets at less than twenty in that South African series. Titmus, with fifty-three Tests in an age when Tests had proliferated, certainly did something to restore the balance, but on the whole the great wicket-takers in county cricket have not had comparable success at Test match level, and this was to be true of Shackleton. In 1950 and 1951 he played for England against South Africa, the West Indies and India – once against each. He did not play for England again until 1963. Then he was recalled for the second Test against the West Indies at Lord's. This was the most gripping Test I have seen. In the first Test, which West Indies won, Brian Statham had taken nought for 121 and had been reluctantly dropped. It was thought that his Test days were done (though as it proved they were not, quite). On the first morning at Lord's, West Indies batting, skies grey and pitch green, it looked a Shackleton day, the kind of day when Hampshire supporters used to rub their hands together, especially at Portsmouth, and mutter about 'Shack's track'. Up till lunch he never bowled a bad ball and never took a wicket. Not till the end of the innings, when he took the last three wickets in four balls, did his figures begin to do justice to his performance. In the match he bowled 84.2 overs, 36 maidens and took 7 for 165. He kept his place in the England side for the rest of the season, but that was all his Test cricket. His relief when at last he took a wicket in that first innings at Lord's was a joy to see. 'It were a bit grim', he said afterwards, 'cooming in for Brian. Couldn't let lads down.'

Shackleton had not really been bowling for Hampshire very long when he seemed to have been bowling for them for ever. He began in 1948 and finished in 1969. An early greyness in his hair soon gave him a venerable aspect. He was 45 when he retired, and such was the strainless economy of his action that he could have gone on for a few more years had he wished. He kept knocking them over for Dorset, and in 1972 was at the top of the Minor Counties' bowling averages. In first-class cricket he took more than a hundred wickets in twenty consecutive seasons. Nobody else has ever done this. Wilfred Rhodes took a hundred wickets in twenty-three seasons, but they were not consecutive.

Shackleton is a Yorkshireman – just. He was born in the Yorkshire part of Todmorden, a town which is half-Lancastrian. We are much the same age, and I might have been brought up in the same town. My father was once invited to the ministry of Todmorden Baptist Church, and nearly accepted. What worried father slightly – or perhaps it was mother – was that the Manse adjoined a cemetery, indeed was almost part of it, and they did not much fancy the idea of little Alan gambolling among the tombs. So we went to Ilkley instead. But young Shackleton as a playmate might have done something for my inswinger.

When he first went to Hampshire, Shackleton brought with him some of the traditional (or traditionally supposed) northern dourness. He regarded his captains, fortunate though he was with them, cautiously. He would say of Desmond Eagar: 'Skipper's idea of dashing bowling tactics is to take me off in 't middle of afternoon, put me on 't other end, and let Vic swan around in 't field for half an hour.' (I must not give the idea that he speaks with a broad Yorkshire accent, but it still comes out in moments of stress.) He mellowed with the years. A grave, gentle person he is now, his character forged in the long, slow fires of a thousand overs, season after season. His son Julian was a useful cricketer, a bowler of much the same style, who never quite fulfilled his promise with Gloucestershire. The burden of father's reputation probably did not help him.

Sir Neville Cardus, some years ago, denied that seam bowling had any technical validity. He maintained that it cannot be explained logically, as spin bowling can be. He was an off-spinner himself and his arguments had some force. But it cannot be wrong to say that Shackleton, even though we think of him as the epitome of the seamer, was a bowler who had length, who had line and (when he chose to employ it) flight. In any phase of cricket's history, these talents would have made him an outstanding bowler.

Hampshire have always been a friendly side. They were forbearing to a brash, not to say cocksure young commentator. But though I have many happy memories of them, few are bibulous. Ingleby-Mackenzie asserted, when they first won the championship in 1961, that they trained on 'wine, women and song', but he had probably the quietest and soberest side in the competition at that time. Since then we have become more accustomed to the championship going the rounds among what we used to think of as the lesser counties, but Hampshire's victory then was only the fifth time in this century that the championship had gone outside the 'Big Six'. I will just point out that Yorkshire, who came second, beat them emphatically in the last match, but that was after the championship was safely won, and there had been some celebrations intervening. I dare say Hampshire were not so quiet and sober that night.

They have won again since, in 1973, and would surely have done so again in 1974, but for some abominable luck with the weather. But they would not thank me for recalling that: the pangs are still too sharp. John Arlott assures me he has never been the same man again, and even the inexhaustibly cheerful Bill Shepheard was beginning to show the strain in those last few days at Bournemouth when the rain went remorselessly on.

I cannot remember when I first met Bill Shepheard. He seemed always to have been part of the Hampshire scenery. He grew high in the counsels of cricket, a member of the Test and County Cricket Board. For Hampshire, no task was too humble for him. He went out of his way to see that visiting pressmen and broadcasters had all the facilities they needed. He had the plumpness which often goes with goodwill, and it was a noble sight to see him and John Arlott at lunchtime, setting about say a cold turkey pie with all trimmings, and a couple of bottles of claret. Bill was best known to the Hampshire public as the man on the public address system. This is a necessary function in modern cricket, especially in Sunday League matches, but it needs a delicate touch, and Bill, genial, informative, but not verbose, did it admirably. I would sometimes mention him in my cricket reports. Indeed, this came to happen so often that once, when I had been watching Hampshire and he did not crop up in *The Times*, I received a letter from a reader expressing the hope that Mr Shepheard was all right. Bill kept these reports in his voluminous scrapbooks. He enjoyed a joke, and had the rare quality of enjoying it all the more if it was his own leg that was being pulled.

Sometimes I gave him merely a passing mention, as at Bournemouth in 1973:

> The New Zealanders must have been pleased to bowl (Hampshire) out for 223, which was ultimately decided to be the figure, after the scoreboards had executed a dashing series of variations which reduced even Bill Shepheard, Hampshire's vastly equable public address man, to some irritation.

Sometimes they were more elaborate, as at Portsmouth in 1974. Hampshire had just beaten Worcestershire (who ultimately overtook them in the championship) in two days.

> Something very unexpected will now have to happen for

Hampshire not to win the championship. Yet although this was a memorable victory, I shall also remember the match for other reasons, not least the adventures of Mr Bill Shepheard, the genial Hampshire announcer.

At the end of the match, for instance, he set the stage for a presentation to the outstanding Hampshire cricketer of the festival, to be made by a Portsmouth garage which was celebrating its jubilee. But when we gathered round the pavilion, there was no presentation. It had not occurred to the innocent mechanics that play might end a day early, and they were far away changing tyres, testing plugs and looking forward to their day out. Mr Shepheard had earlier announced that a white boy's sweater had been found. Later, he announced that a wallet had been found. My colleague Mr Rutnagur, who is an Indian, ventured to enquire whether it was a white man's wallet.

But Mr Shepheard's best moment came when he said: 'Play has been resumed in the Test match – oh, and by the way, President Nixon has resigned.' The cheer, a mixture of irony, relief and scorn, brought a man running out of the bar, thinking that another wicket had gone. When he discovered it was nothing so important, he went back in again. Thus do the mighty fall.

Then, from a report of a match at Basingstoke, when Hampshire were eighty for six against Sussex:

The relative recovery thereafter sprang from Gilliat, who always looks a high class batsman when he is in form. He played Snow well. Let us hope he can strike the same vein against the fast bowlers of the West Indies at the weekend. It was his 32nd birthday, we were informed by Bill Shepheard, zealous as ever on the public address system. He was so carried away by emotion (Bill Shepheard, not Richard Gilliat) that he went on to give us details of what is obviously an important new competition, the Ben Player Cup.

An incident at Bournemouth:

The pitch gave the bowlers some help after the rain, though not all that much. I inspected it at tea time with a colleague. It looked like any other second day pitch to me, but my friend brought out prongs and cocktail sticks and conducted scientific tests upon it. I should explain that he is a member of the TCCB Pitches Committee. We were hoping, vainly, to raise a shout from the Hampshire announcer, Bill Shepheard ('Boys, will you please keep off the square?')

Tony Lewis will remember the occasion. It was the day we made the acquaintance of the weakened inner wall of Jesty's lower abdomen. Jesty had explained in these technical terms the reason for his withdrawal from the match, and I was so taken by this example of your modern professional's conversational style (compare Goddard, T. 'I done me gut'), that I had something of an abdominal seizure myself.

There was, soon afterwards, great excitement at Southampton, with a Gillette Cup semi-final coming up:

This event has caught the imagination of the county, and presents the organisers with the largest attendance problem of their lives. Desmond Eagar is paling under his tan. Even Bill Shepheard's voice, as he announces all the complicated arrangements for getting tickets, quavers a little – though that did not stop a woman living nearby from ringing to complain of the noise of the public address system. This was unfair to Shepheard, whose announcements are always witty, restrained and informative. Still, he rang the woman back, and looks forward to welcoming her at the next John Player League match. Now that he has lost so much weight, there is no telling what the good Shepheard will be up to next.

That was in August, 1976. In May, I wrote this in my weekly journal for *The Cricketer*:

At Bournemouth, where I went for the Benson and Hedges match against Somerset, I was saddened to hear of the death of Bill Shepheard. He was not so young, and had been ill, but it came as a shock, for he was never a man to give in. I was told that only a few days before his death he had struggled to get up the steps to the announcer's box, just to see if he could do it, but found that he could not. Bill was, in many different capacities, a strength and stay of cricket, especially Hampshire cricket, and the kindest of friends. He was buried last week, with his MCC tie, his Hampshire tie, and his Hampshire membership card. If you think this funny or sentimental, by all means laugh about it. Bill would not mind . . . Ah, happy days, and how I shall miss you at the Hampshire grounds, dear Bill.

Desmond Eagar paid an eloquent tribute to Bill at a memorial service, and died himself in the following September. Hampshire cricket has never, for me, been quite the same.

IX
Lesser Breeds within the Law

'Cowslips from a Devon combe'
Kipling, The Flowers

'Going up Camborne hill coming down'
old Cornish song

Not often now do I see a Minor Counties' match, though the Minor Counties have been very much a part of my cricketing life. The last championship match I saw was, I think in 1974, when I travelled to Camborne to watch the second day of the match between Cornwall and Devon. A remarkable game it was, or at least it contained a remarkable player. Cornwall had scored 175 in the first innings. Devon had been bowled out for sixty-two, Halfyard taking seven wickets. It was a surprise to see Halfyard playing for Cornwall, though I suppose it should not have been. He is one of the indestructibles, a kind of English Bill Alley, whom he resembles in physique, bowling action and humour. He played for Surrey, Kent, Nottinghamshire and Durham before he arrived in Cornwall. He had also had a spell as a first-class umpire, when his career with Kent – and it seemed his entire playing career – was ended by a severe motor accident. Motor accidents have inter-rupted and in some cases concluded the lives of more first-class cricketers than is proportionately justifiable. Hesitate before you accept a lift from a cricketer.

There was Halfyard at 43 still cutting them off a damp Camborne pitch. He was qualified for Cornwall because he had become professional to the Holman's club. Cornwall declared their second innings on the Saturday afternoon. Devon never looked like getting the runs; it was a question of whether they could save the match. It also became a question of whether Halfyard would take all ten wickets. He had the first six out, the total ninety-three and every fieldsman within ten yards of the bat. If a Devon batsman played towards mid-off, Halfyard had to turn and run after the ball himself. He followed through a long way, and was not so fast when he chased. Never have gentler forward defensive pushes more readily earned three runs.

As the game went on, I was beginning to have a personal problem. My duty at Camborne was to report for the *The Sunday Times*. *The Sunday Times* likes its cricket reports early. Indeed, it likes them best if you can send a 'complete rounded report' between the time the captains toss in the morning and the beginning of play. At the latest, they want their rounded reports by tea. So on this day I had telephoned my report by teatime, and all that remained was a little tidying up at the end, which was scheduled for six o'clock. At 6.10 a train was due to leave Camborne, which I had to catch. It was the last train which would enable me to reach Swansea the following day to cover a match for *The Times* (quite a different animal, you understand). A Cornish friend undertook to send through the close of play score, and a sentence or two, on my behalf. But Cornwall were obviously going to claim the extra half hour – and suppose Halfyard took all ten wickets? More than a sentence or two would be required. It seemed to me that I would be getting into trouble with either John Lovesey (then sports editor of *The Sunday Times*) or John Hennessey (then sports editor of *The Times*). I suppose I was more scared of Hennessey than Lovesey. I ordered a taxi and caught the train. When I left the result was still open. Halfyard had taken all eight wickets that had fallen. It was with some concern that I looked up the result the next day, but my luck was in. The match ended in a draw, and though Devon had lost one more wicket, Halfyard had not taken it.

A week or two after this, however, he did take all ten wickets in an innings, and all sixteen which Cornwall captured in the match against Dorset at Penzance. He was awarded a case of champagne by *The Sunday Telegraph* as their cricketer of the week. Cornwall came second in the championship that year, but could only draw with Oxfordshire in the 'challenge match'. These matches have rarely been much fun because the challenged side knows from the start that a draw will be sufficient. The weather was bad at Oxford which cost some time. In their second innings, with everyone waiting for a declaration, they batted nearly four hours for 194 for 6, before setting Cornwall to score 288 in 70 minutes. During Oxfordshire's second innings, Halfyard bowled underarm, and then three donkey-drops in an over. His captain, Laity, replaced him and bowled with his left arm, not his usual one. This was all rather disagreeable. But Halfyard took seventy-four wickets that season, and headed the averages for the Minor Counties.

The Minor Counties' championship has a long history, but it has declined in public appeal. The gap between its standards and those of the first-class game gradually widened with the spread of professionalism. You will find a good account of the atmosphere in a Minor Counties' match early in this century, in the great days, in *The Hampdenshire Wonder*, by J. D. Beresford. (A marvellous book which you should read anyway.) It is almost impossible now to imagine a Minor Counties player picked for England, as Barnes was when he was playing for Staffordshire, or Chapman from Berkshire, or D. C. H. Townsend from Durham. When the second eleven competition for first-class counties was introduced, with the consequent removal of most second elevens from the Minor Counties championship, I thought we should see a return to gaiety: more genuine county spirit, fewer young professionals, their eyes only on a first team place, concentrating on their averages. But this does not seem to have happened. Two-day matches are still begun as if they were five-day Tests. The proportion of drawn matches remains high, even in a dry summer.

Cricket originated in Cornwall I have been told: as well as football, and steam engines, and china clay, and tin, and cream, and pasties, and Methodism. The Cornish are inclined to be a little Russo-American in their claims for inventing things. Major Rowland Bowen, in his *Cricket: A History of its Growth and Development Throughout the World* (Eyre & Spottiswoode, 1977) finds many possible sources for the origins of the game, including Celtic ones, but does not mention Cornwall. Since he lived in his latter years at Mullion, the evidence for Cornwall cannot be strong. However, there is a theory – I think it was Edmund Blunden who put it forward – that the first known cricket match was played between the Irish giant Cuchullain and a Hundred Colts of Ulster. The score was,

Colts, b Cuchullain	0
Cuchullain, not out	1

Now Cuchullain was related to the Giant Bolster, who once reigned over West Cornwall. Bolster was six miles high, and would stand with one foot on Carn Brea and the other on St Agnes Beacon, peering benevolently down upon his people (you will find a splendid picture of him, and some notes on his career, in *Popular Romances of the West of England*, by Robert Hunt, FRS, illustrated by George Cruickshank, first published in 1864). What more natural than that Cuchullain should have confided a few details of this interesting new game to his Cornish cousin? This is the best case I can put up for cricket originating in Cornwall. But despite the giant's august blessings, Cornwall have still never won the Minor Counties' championship.

In 1969 Cornwall made their first appearance in the Gillette Cup. There would have been a big crowd at Truro, but it rained all Saturday. When the match did take place, spread over two damp days, it had become an anticlimax. But Glamorgan, who had spent a cheerful weekend in Cornish hostelries, were at one time sixty-two for four, and Tony Lewis was so moved when one of his batsmen was given out, caught on the boundary, when the fieldsman was behind the ropes (the crowd patriotically standing clear), that he went on to the field himself to protest to the umpire. The umpire was Bill Alley. I would have given much to be a witness of this meeting, but after a wasted Saturday I had gone home. I have, however, interviewed both participants, and their accounts of the conversation agree.

> **Alley** (seeing captain on field). Captain!
> **Lewis** Er . . .
> **Alley** (conclusively): Captain, – – – – off.

Glamorgan won easily enough in the end, though Tony still winces when you remind him of the occasion.

There have been some good Cornish cricketers who played for other counties. Richards, the Surrey wicket-keeper, is the most recent. He was born at Penzance, and educated at the famous Humphry Davy School. Harris, first of Middlesex and then of Nottinghamshire, was near the England side. He never had so to speak a Cornish aspect. He was taken professional young, and acquired the usual accent of young professionals seeking to make their way in the modern world, what Cardus once called 'the purest Teddington'. But he was a pretty good batsman, and he was born at St Just-in-Roseland, in the lovely Roseland peninsula, where the green banks of the churchyard slope down into the sea. I must here tell you of an incident which happened many years ago. About a mile and a half from the village of St Just-in-Roseland is a signpost, which says, emphatically, 'BAR'. Ralph Wightman and Denzil Batchelor, who were walking together in the interests of a radio programme, turned down the lane, following the sign, one hot summer morning. Neither of them were at that time of their lives great walkers, but the lure of the sign was irresistible. It is (or was) the *harbour* bar to which the sign refers. By the time they had retraced their steps, the pubs were shut. I tell the tale as I was told. I can vouch for the existence of the misleading signpost.

The Cornish origins of Harris were acknowledged in his nickname 'Pasty', but he did not play much in Cornwall. The best Cornish batsman of those years (I mean in the sense of playing for Cornwall) was G. R. Harvey, the leader of the Minor Counties' averages in 1969, a Blundell's boy who could have made a professional career had he so wished. Harvey came from St Columb Major.

From St Columb Major too came Jack Crapp, who must be the best cricketer Cornwall has so far produced. It was in the late 1930s that we began to hear reports of a new young batsman in the Gloucestershire side whom good judges expected to play for England. They were proved right, though Crapp was a little slow to develop. In 1938 he scored 1700 runs, and *Wisden* commented that 'he would have improved further by the more general use of his natural aptitude to force the game'. It makes odd reading for those of us who only became familiar with him in the postwar years, when he frequently lost his wicket through genial attempts to hoick the spinners over long-on (he was a left-hander). Before the war, Gloucestershire had Hammond and Barnett to go for the runs, and Crapp's function was to provide solid support in the middle of the order.

He had a mediocre season in 1946, which removed any chance of his accompanying Hammond's team to Australia. But after the Australians had won the first two 1948 Tests by wide margins, Crapp was picked for the third. He gave himself a workout with a hundred against them at Bristol. In the Test match he played a sound innings of thirty-seven at a time when England were in trouble. He was leg-before to Lindwall, but it was Arlott who really got him out. All day we had been reassured by the commentators that batsman after England batsman was settling in comfortably, or words to that effect. No sooner was such a thing said than the man was out. An agonised listener sent a telegram to the ground, begging them not to say such a thing again, on the tempting-providence principle. John Arlott read out the telegram admitting its force and could not help adding, 'But I'm sure Jack Crapp's going to get some runs.' That was the end of Jack. However, he kept his place to the end of the series (as did John) and went to South Africa that winter under F. G. Mann. He did well there, averaging nearly forty in the Tests, and over fifty in all matches.

The next season, in England, he made over 2000 runs, and it is a little perplexing that those two series were the limit of his Test career. I suppose he began to lose mobility in the field. But he continued to play very well for Gloucestershire, and became a Test match umpire. He lived most of his life in Bristol, but never forgot his Cornish origins. He was a warm man, warmly loved. At his funeral in 1981, with many distinguished cricketers attending, the closing hymn was 'The Old Rugged Cross', which, despite its unfortunate associations in America with the Ku Klux Klan, was always a Cornish favourite.

Moving across the Tamar into Devon, it occurs to me that this is the moment to say something of my own cricket, most of which was played there. I do so only because old friends will otherwise point out the omission: as it is, they take pleasure in saying how extraordinary it is that such a poor cricketer should have stumbled into such an occupation. But here I will defend myself a little. I had no real talent for the game, but by taking pains I developed into a tolerable club cricketer. I once, in a house match at Taunton, took five wickets in five balls, and not many cricketers can say that. The batsmen are, I trust, alive to say if I lie. I had long legs and could go down the pitch and drive the ball over the bowler's head, now and then. I was captain of my college at Oxford and played a few times for the Authentics, probably for social reasons. I also scored many noughts, and had plenty of nought for eighty-sevens. These are the performances my friends remember, callously and perhaps a touch jealously. But I was just about good enough for the game to be more of a joy than a misery. I had to stop playing regularly in my late twenties when I joined the BBC, and was usually working on

Saturday afternoons. But I continued to play as often as I could: on mid-week evenings I would cheerfully go, to make up the number, to any club in the neighbourhood. At one time and another, I must have had a game – not necessarily in the first eleven – at nearly all the clubs in South Devon, and there are a lot of them. So there, and take it out of that.

Devon have only won the championship once, in 1978, long after I had left there, but club cricket has always been strong. There was a tragedy in 1955. Devon came second in the table, challenged Surrey II, and were full of confidence as they went to the Oval led by Grahame Parker. It rained a good deal. Between the showers Surrey scored 236 for 8 and declared. When Devon batted H. D. Fairclough, who had taken 4 for 46, scored 117. There was no chance of a definite result, but Parker claimed the extra half hour, anxious for at least the moral victory of first innings points. There was some misunderstanding and the players left the field, but Grahame is a pertinacious and knowledgeable man when it comes to a point of cricket law, and in the end he was allowed to take it. So though they had no championship, Devon had demonstrated the quality of their side. Moderate rejoicing in Totnes and Tiverton.

But then, as I remember hearing it lucidly expressed, they done it on us. Under Rule 16 of the competition, the points obtained from the game were added to the table of results, and the percentages of both counties recalculated. Surrey remained in first place, but Devon were put down to fourth behind Bucking-hamshire and Nottinghamshire II. To realise how absurd this was, you need only reflect that it might easily have happened under such a system that Surrey might also have dropped a place or two. We could thus have had a situation when neither competitor in the challenge match won the championship, and Buckinghamshire, without either challenging or being challenged, would have been victors.

At the AGM of the Minor Counties, there was a move to record the match as 'No Result'. It is hard to see how this, on the face of it, would have helped. It would simply have deprived Devon of a further point. I imagine that the intention of the proposal was simply that the game should not be included in the final table. The proposal was rejected, and rightly so since it would have been retrospective legislation. The mischief was a ridiculous rule in the first place. A resolution of sympathy with Devon was unanimously passed, distantly accompanied by snorts of disgust from *The White*

Hart at Exeter to *The Leaping Salmon* at Horrabridge. The rule was changed the following season, so that the positions of the teams taking part in the challenge match are unaffected, unless the challengers win outright. This was what the rule had been twenty years before. It is a classic example, far from the only one in the regulation of cricket, of superfluous administrative meddling.

Only a few years ago someone in Devon was reminding me of the time when Grahame Parker 'lost Devon the championship by claiming the extra half hour'. This was a slander on Grahame. The facts were sad enough as they stood.

I must say a word or two more about him, though, if only because he is an old friend. He was not so young at the time of that match, but had been an outstanding sportsman in the 1930s. He played full-back for England three times at rugby, and for Gloucester, Gloucestershire and the Barbarians (four Cambridge Blues, 1932–35). He is a Gloucestershire man from the Crypt School. He was a schoolmaster, first at Dulwich, then for many years at Blundell's (which gave him his Devon qualification). When he retired from Blundell's, he became secretary of the Gloucestershire County Cricket Club, a post he occupied for some years to general satisfaction. His only weakness, that I remember, was that before he went on the public address system (he was a little distrustful of these modern inventions) he would blow into it several times to make sure it was working. This caused me to give him the name 'Puff, the Magic Dragon'. Thereafter, if he knew I was on the ground, he would give an extra puff. He won cricket Blues in 1934 and 1935, captain in 1935. He played for Gloucestershire almost always when school duties permitted, from 1932 to 1951. But until he decided to leave Blundell's, teaching was the greater part of his life. He must have been a very good schoolmaster, and a very good sports coach as well. Richard Sharp has written of how he was helped by him. I remember very well Richard's first rugby international against Wales at Twickenham, when he played a blinder and the press was full of his praise, enough to turn a young man's head and spoil him for ever. Grahame wrote to him, 'You will be very much a marked man from now on and life will get much tougher for you. You will have less room and will get thumped harder and more often.' Richard adds, 'These were the words to listen to.' Many other young footballers and cricketers have been grateful to Grahame's wise words, encouraging in bad times, calming in good.

But writing about Grahame has taken me some way from Devon. They had another good season in 1968, when they again finished second, and could have challenged Yorkshire II. They did not choose to challenge, partly because of a feeling that those up-along slickers would diddle them again. They did, however, by their success, qualify for the Gillette Cup for the first time. They played Hertfordshire at Stevenage and were beaten by ninety-eight runs in a match spread over three days because of rain. Before the match they received a telegram:

AND ALL WHO SAIL IN HER
DAVID SHEPHERD, GLOUCESTERSHIRE

David Shepherd, born in Northam, near Bideford, had scored hundreds of runs for Devon before he joined Gloucestershire in 1965. He became a kind of symbol of Devon cricket, so ruddy, tubby, good-humoured, a natural hitter. He scored a century in his first match for Gloucestershire, 108 out of 139. (Looking up the account of this match in *Wisden*, I see it is recorded that 'Martin, the Oxford captain, had to rest because of a boil.') It was not the first time that Oxford bowlers had had to rest because of a boil. The great T.E.B. was so known. Shepherd was, however, a different kind of irritant. His first century was a mixed blessing to him. He had to learn that the first-class game was not so easy as all that. He had to work hard for his county cap, but he did a lot for Gloucestershire.

'Let me have men about me that are fat', is not the usual prayer of a cricket captain, but there have been plenty of fine players built on substantial lines. I remember how astonished I was by the bulk of Richard Tyldesley, a Lancashire and England spinner, not much past his peak when I saw him. Armitage of Yorkshire, who played in the very first Test match (and enabled Bannerman to score the decisive century, by dropping a simple catch) was a man who was remembered for a notable waistline, which had widened after a few months of Antipodean hospitality. Maurice Leyland was a fleet outfield in his youth but can never have been exactly spare in build, and in his last seasons, after the war, had an adipose look. It is said that Leyland once set out on a long run at the Oval, from slip towards third man (none placed), the ball going to the Vauxhall end, and as he departed his captain, Brian Sellers, cried 'Save seven!' And then there was W.G., a champion over hurdles in his youth, who became so heavy that when at last he was dropped from the England side (aged 51) it was less for batting deficiencies than because he could not bend quickly any more, and a Trent Bridge crowd had actually jeered him.

David Shepherd's only rival – for size – in the county cricket of his time, was Colin Milburn. Milburn was the better batsman, but Shepherd was the better fieldsman. I have known him say, with quiet confidence, that he would be happy to take Milburn on over a hundred yards, and he would certainly have carried my money. I remember a tremendous run in the outfield which cut off what seemed a sure four in a Benson & Hedges final.

There was a time when David got a little too fat and was slowing up. He tightened himself in the winter in Devon, possibly by abstaining from oggies and beer, possibly by training with the rugby lads (he had been a good rugby player in his youth, at the improbable position of scrum-half). Anyway, he has kept himself in good shape since, given his appetite and his metabolism, if that is the right word. As an umpire, he gives a man out with a swift upthrusting finger, like thunder 'crost the bay. No umpire of my time has been more emphatic.

As for his batting, he became famous for what at Bristol I have heard described as a 'Shepresc' – abbreviation for a Shepherd rescue. I do not think he ever much enjoyed going in at 270 for 3. He much preferred going in at 27 for 3 with the challenge to put things right. He was soon joined in the Gloucestershire side by another Devonian, Jack Davey from Tavistock.

You may sometimes, at a Gloucestershire match, observe a bright blue tie with a silver inscription, 'J.J?' The wearer will be a member of the 'J.J?' Society. These are its origins.

Jack has only one Christian name. One day his captain, Tony Brown, felt that this was a little unfair on him, as everybody else had two initials. So they popped in an extra J. This was repeated on scorecards up and down the country for some time. Speculation grew, encouraged I fear by a mischievous journalist, as to what the extra J. stood for. Jolly Jack? Jocose Jack? Jovial Jack? Jubilee Jack? Jocund Jack? Jesting Jack? Jabbering Jack? Jaunty Jack? Jumping Jack? Hence the query on the tie of his fan club. The members, strictly limited to twenty-five, are required to wear the tie on certain days of the season, including Jack's birthday, and hold an annual dinner to celebrate his Jovian name. When he was playing and went to bat, their duty was to cheer loudly. Favoured expressions were 'Put them to the sword, Jack!' and 'Cold steel, Jack!' I was once present, the only member at Folkestone or it may have been Dover, when Jack went in. After taking the precaution of leaving the press box, I gave the best roar of which I was capable. Severe Kentish looks were directed at me. I rather think one of them came from Jim Swanton. But I had fulfilled my constitutional duty. Jack was more startled than anyone, at the familiar hail so far from home, and got out immediately.

No, he was not much of a batsman. David Green recalls a match with Leicestershire when Gloucestershire needed seven runs, and Leicestershire one wicket, with an over to go for a final first innings point. Jack had to play the last four balls. He pushed forward carefully at three, missing two (the appropriate J.J? cry in these circumstances was 'Well left, Jack') and then tried to hit the last one for seven, and was caught at mid-off. But he did once score fifty-three, not out, sharing a stand of ninety-nine with Shepherd at Bristol in 1977. One of the J.J? members present was a butcher from the Forest of Dean, who had his van with him. He presented Jack, on the field, with a frozen lamb. I wish I had been there.

Jack was a pretty good bowler, though he never became quite so good as most of us expected. Fastish left-arm bowlers are less uncommon than they used to be, but still comparative rarities, and they usually have a better chance of reaching the heights than your right-armers, who if short of the highest pace can easily dwindle into routine seamers. When I first saw Jack, I thought he might develop into another Nobby Clark (who did much service for Northamptonshire and England). Occasional injuries, not usually too serious in themselves but coming at awkward times, affected his career. His action, springy and finely balanced, needed only a slight physical handicap to disturb it. If he tried to battle through a strain, he would lose his rhythm. If he rested for a while, he could not easily recapture it. When he was younger, he was less liable to strains, but was too inexperienced to make full use of his talents. As he grew older, he became a more thoughtful, subtler bowler, but the years had made their demands. It is the story familiar to us all, but especially fast bowlers: 'Si jeunese savoit; si vieillese pouvoit'. Jack's physique was never ideal for his job. Most of the best fast bowlers have had big bottoms. I know there was Statham, but there you are dealing with genius. It is a pity that David Shepherd's waistline was not more like Jack's, and Jack's bottom more like David's. But Devon could be proud of them both.

There have been lots of other good Devon cricketers, notably in recent years the Tolchard brothers from Torquay (Roger Tolchard played four times for England). But I resist the temptation to choose an all-time Devon eleven. There are, however, two more cricketing episodes in the county's cricketing history to which I must refer, one ancient and one modern.

The early Australian sides used to land at Plymouth, and sometimes play a match or two while finding their land legs. The 1882 Australians (the first to win a Test in England) landed there. One of their batsmen was G. J. Bonnor. He played 17 times against England in the period 1880 to 1888, and as he made 512 runs at an average of 17, you could not call him, even by the scoring standards of his time, an outstanding success. But he was an exceptionally strong man, with a great reputation as a hitter, and a thrower.

On the voyage over, Bonnor made a bet that he would throw a cricket ball 110 yards, *first throw on landing*. The last was the essential clause after weeks at sea. As soon as they had left the ship, the Australians drove to the premises of William Hearder, a Plymouth business man, who had been recommended to them as an impartial judge. He took them to the Mount Wise ground, but it was slippery and Bonnor said that he would prefer a hard surface. So they went to the parade ground of Raglan Barracks. The distance was marked off by newspapers. Hearder handed Bonnor an ordinary match ball, and held the stakes, two cheques for £100.

Bonnor did not run. He threw from where he stood. 'It seemed', wrote Hearder, 'as if the ball would never stop rising.' The distance was measured at 119 yards, 5 inches. Bonnor promptly offered double or quits that his next throw would be over 125 yards, but there were no takers.

According to *Wisden* for 1982 (fortified by some interesting research in the columns of *The Cricketer*) the longest recorded throw was by Robert Percival on Durham Racecourse in 1884, 140 yards 2 feet. Eight years earlier Ross Mackenzie had thrown 140 yards 9 inches at Toronto. In 1876, even more remarkably, W. F. Forbes, aged 18, threw 132 yards at the Eton College sports. Throwing the cricket ball was then a principal feature of school sports days, and all these were achieved with much preparation and practice. I cannot believe that, given the circumstances, there has ever been a more astonishing throw than Bonnor's at Raglan Barracks. Certainly the memory lasted long: seventy years later I was shown the site. It is well authenticated. Hearder describes it in a letter to W. G. Grace, and his account is confirmed by George Giffen, who was also present.

The modern episode on which I touch is the Torquay Festival, which began in 1954. Devon have several times aspired to first-class status, and part of the thinking behind the festival was to demonstrate that such an ambition was feasible. Since it lasted for only five years it failed to make that particular point, but provided some happy times while it lasted. It took some courage to start it, because first-class cricket was becoming a dubious proposition anywhere then, when the postwar boom had faded, and before football pools, one-day competitions and sponsorship were summoned in aid. I believe it was Harold Gimblett who first had the idea. Ben Brockman, a local enthusiast, took it up, and David Haines was appointed secretary.

David was the brother of that C. V. L. Haines who had been so remarkably caught by our present ambassador in Jeddah. He was a slow left-armer who played a lot for Devon. Once I saw him in a county match have three chances dropped off his bowling, from three consecutive balls, by the same fieldsman at long-off. That was at Torquay, and no doubt gave him a resignation in the face of punishment which stood him in good stead in the festival days. David became one of my warmest friends in cricket, and I do not forgive myself that I missed his funeral where I had been asked to say a few words. The roads were icy, and I was directed to the wrong church, but I still feel ashamed.

At first the festival, with a subsidy from the Council, went well. In the second year there was a small profit. But the weather turned unkind even for English Septembers. Five and a half days out of six were lost one year. And in 1958, when the weather was reasonably good, there was another heavy loss. One morning in bright sunshine Worrell and Sobers were batting, two of the most attractive stroke-makers in the world. Lock was bowling to them, and Lock never enjoyed being hit, festival or no. The ground was about one-third full. George Emmett, who was playing in the match, and had been professional at Torquay in days when you might have expected as big a crowd for a club match, turned to David Haines and said ruefully: 'What do they want? Good heavens, what *do* they want?' What they wanted, though the thought seemed blasphemous then, was one-day cricket. Somerset have filled the ground there with Sunday League matches. It has sometimes occurred to me that the festival might be revived, on a limited scale, with a west country equivalent of the Fenner Trophy at Scarborough. Gloucestershire, Somerset, a combined Devon and Cornwall side, and either Hampshire or Glamorgan might take part. A sponsor could conceivably find it worth while.

I still have a Torquay Festival tie, which must be on the way to becoming a rarity. I was involved because the West of England Home Service broadcast commentary on most of the matches. We had a good deal of fun. Maurice Tremlett's midnight non-bathe was not the only one I remember. On one occasion the party was led by A. C. D. Ingleby-Mackenzie who decided to go to some distant beach beyond Babbacombe. There were four cars, and the car park, which could take about four hundred, was totally empty when we arrived. Nevertheless an attendant suddenly emerged from his darkened sentry box, and not only charged us but insisted that the cars were meticulously lined up side by side in a distant corner. There was a famous bet between Willie Jones and Ted Dickinson. Ted was an amply built member of the local committee. Willie played cricket for Glamorgan, and rugby for Gloucestershire, a fly-half who would have played for a country less well endowed with them than Wales. Willie maintained, upon a glass or two, that he could throw a rugby ball further than Ted could kick it. Spurred on, he declared that he could throw a *reverse pass* further than Ted could kick a ball. The day's play was over, and we all trooped on to the field so that the question could be tested. Three reverse throws were allowed against three kicks, longest to count. A book was quickly made. I backed Willie, but he lost – by a foot.

I remember, too, the furious series of matches played one night at the Cott Inn, Dartington. These were not cricket, but table football. Sam Mearing, the landlord (a considerable sportsman in several ways) and his barmaid Joan, who were nearly invincible on their own table, represented England. C. L. McCool and V. E. Jackson represented Australia. The Australians lost fourteen times running. The night was now well advanced, but they declared they were not departing until they had won. They won next time. We were just going, when they became suspicious that their victory had been a fiddle, and it started all over again.

I used to watch Dorset, sometimes, and Wiltshire. Dorset seemed a particularly happy side, especially when D. J. W. Bridge was captain. Derek Bridge had been a contemporary of mine at

Oxford, a Blue and an England trialist at rugby. I may be doing him an injustice, but I think the only first-class cricket match in which he played was in 1947, not for the university, but for Northamptonshire against the South Africans. Northamptonshire were missing an opening bowler, or possibly two, and had summoned him at short notice. He did not have much success, and on the third morning was back in the Parks watching Oxford. 'Ah, Derek', said somebody cruelly, 'Finished them off in two days, I see.' But he made a splendid Dorset captain. M. M. Walford batted well for Dorset in his later cricketing years. But the finest innings I ever saw played for them was by the Reverend G. L. O. Jessop, against Cornwall at Camborne. He is the son of G.L., and was getting towards venerability at the time I saw him, but I felt I had had a glimpse even at second-hand, of the magic.

Dorset have never won the Minor Counties' championship, but Wiltshire have, twice, both before the first war. They might have won again in 1933, but for one of those endearing muddles which from time to time have rippled the placid surface of the competition.

If you look at the list of champions, you will see that in that year the championship goes down as 'undecided'. This was what happened. At the end of the season the published table of results showed that Norfolk were first, with a percentage of 72.00, followed by Yorkshire II, with 71.66. Yorkshire challenged, and won at Norwich by nine wickets. Nearly two months passed. When the table was being checked for insertion in *Wisden* it was noticed that some of the figures disagreed. There was an investigation, and it was discovered that when Yorkshire had played Staffordshire in July, they had been credited with points for a win in a one-day match (5) instead of points for a win on the first innings (3). This reduced Yorkshire's percentage from 71.66 to 68.33, which would have put them in third place below Wiltshire. They therefore had no right to challenge: but they had done so and won. It was decided to ignore the so-called challenge match, but as it was by now the end of October, it was too late for Wiltshire to challenge. It was no more than a silly mistake, but in Wiltshire cricketing circles it was regarded as an example of the usual skulduggery upalong. They had another good run in the 1960s, helped by several Marlborough masters. The best batsman I recall seeing play for them was David Turner, born in Chippenham, who after a season left to join Hampshire. He has certainly not been a failure for

Hampshire, but never quite fulfilled a promise which many thought exceptional.

The last match I have seen between Minor Counties was between Devon and Cornwall at Exeter in 1980. Editors scarcely bother to notice the scores nowadays. However, I persuaded mine to let me go, because it was the first round of the Gillette Cup, and the only chance I was ever likely to have of seeing them in a quasi-senior match. Furthermore, it had been hinted that Jack Davey might be playing, so I put on my blue and silver tie and prepared myself to give the J.J? salute.

The match itself was disappointing, Devon winning too easily. It was a quiet occasion. I was struck again by the different atmosphere from an encounter between these two counties at rugby. Large crowds assemble for the rugby matches, feelings run high. For many years I broadcast commentary on them, and always received much correspondence afterwards. This could be divided into two piles, one saying, more or less, 'You Cornish basket', and the other 'You Devon clod'. It is not at all like that at the cricket. The Exeter ground was a pleasant, peaceful place to be, with warm sunshine, a noble view of the Haldon Hills and Dunchideock Castle. There were numerous old friends. Jack Davey turned up in the afternoon, and I am sure would have loved to have been playing, though as it happened Devon had no need of him. Jack had by then taken over *The Devil's Elbow* at Princetown, and I rather fear it may have opened a little late that evening.

I thought, as I travelled home in the evening, through the incomparable sunlit countryside of the west, that I had not often had a happier day at the cricket.

X
Lights unto my Path

'A word spoken in due season, how good is it!'
Proverbs, xv, 23

I must have spent as much time reading about cricket as playing it or watching it. In my youth I would read any cricket book that came my way, even instructional textbooks which meant little to me. I still read about it a lot, though so much is now published on the game that I have to be more selective, and do not bother with the ghosted autobiographies of modern players – a ghosted autobiography before, say, 1900, while usually intrinsically as valueless as the modern ones, has by now acquired a certain antique vitality of its own.

The first proper book I remember reading about cricket, when I was aged 7 or 8, was *The Story of the Tests*. I do not know who wrote it, but I am grateful to him. It was published at the price of sixpence, in a series by 'The London Book Company', under the aegis of Collins: hard maroon back, but poor quality paper and binding. I bought it in Woolworth's, with a dust jacket which had pictures of the triumphant English side which toured Australia in 1928–29. I read it so intensely that the binding soon came off.

Half the book was about the 1928–29 series, though there was also a long account of the famous victory at the Oval in 1926. By the time I read it, those victories had become a little soured because of the terrible things Bradman had done to us in 1930. But I was able to keep a sense of perspective because of the earlier part of the book, a history of Tests between England and Australia. I could still quote passages from it: for instance 'In most people's opinion, so far as Test cricket was concerned, Wilfred Rhodes was decidedly on the shelf.' 'The Lion's tail was indeed well up!' 'The Colt flung up his hands as he realised the impossibility of saving the four.'

The Colt (I think I am correct about the capital C) was Bradman, and it was the hit by Geary which won the Ashes. A. E. R. Gilligan was regularly misprinted A. E. R. Gillingham, something which baffled me for years. I bless that book. I set to work with my lead soldiers, replaying some of the less satisfactory series of the past. When I had done with it, 1921 was a much better season for England.

The next book that made a major impact upon me was *Ayres' Public Schools Cricket Companion* for the year 1932. I was not a public schoolboy, and such a prospect had not then entered my head, but I thought I knew about public schools because I read Frank Richards and Talbot Baines Reed, and I was entranced by *Ayres*. It cost 2s 6d hard-backed. Rather surprisingly, in retrospect, I never had a *Wisden* until 1937. For several years I kept asking for *Ayres* as a birthday present, but although father dutifully tried, he could never find one. I only discovered the reason for this when, in 1970, I was reading Rowland Bowen's history. He writes, of the early part of the twentieth century,

> School cricket in this period meant public school cricket: this was a period when a young man would stay on until he was nineteen or even twenty, in order to play for his team, and if he could establish a reputation thereby, obtain a place in University despite a poor scholastic record. It had a following amongst the public too, and was able to command commercially worthwhile sales for a cricket annual largely devoted to public schools.

In a footnote, Major Bowen identifies *Ayres*: first issue 1902, last 1932. So my copy of *Ayres* was the last. It is no use wishing I had kept it. Once again my fierce and repeated assaults soon had the covers off and the pages falling apart. There was an article by Bradman, reprinted from *Don Bradman's Book* (this was the book – much slighter than his later works – which caused Bradman to be fined for breach of contract by the Australian Board of Control). There was – the most fascinating part to me – a 'Who's Who' of the county cricketers of the time. And there were long reports on the principal matches of the public schools, many of them reprinted from school magazines; and the results and averages of any school which could possibly, in the terminology of those days, describe itself as 'public'. I can still tell you without checking a good deal about the public school cricket of 1931. Eton beat Harrow by an innings. The Eton innings was opened by N. S. Hotchkin and A. W. Allen, both of whom scored centuries. It was a record first-wicket partnership for the match. Repton were easily beating Malvern, but the match had to be abandoned because of rain on the second day, and then the sun came out and shone on the backs of the retreating Malvernians: this, I am pretty sure, was the phrase used in *The Reptonian*, though it now occurs to me that as the Malvernians were travelling westwards, the sun can hardly have shone on their *backs*. Eton had a narrow win over Winchester. Cheltenham trounced Haileybury.

I took sides in all these matches. I was on Harrow's side against Eton, perhaps because Harrow had not won for so long. I was very pleased when, in 1939, they won at Lord's after thirty-one years. I was on Repton's side against Malvern, and felt quite as deeply as the correspondent of *The Reptonian* that it was a shame Malvern had got away with it. My favourite school was Winchester, and I could not understand why they did not play at Lord's, not knowing the complicated history of the matter. It seemed to me shocking that while Winchester were barred, two such relatively unknown schools as Beaumont and Oratory did. Father suggested darkly, and not altogether inaccurately, that this must be something to do with the Pope.

I replayed these matches, when necessary, not only with my soldiers, but sometimes with my schoolmates on the stone playground of Farmer Road School. Armed with the information of *Ayres*, I would allocate the principal parts. But unlike my soldiers, my schoolmates were not under my control. However carefully I chose the sides, you could never tell what would happen. In the Eton/Harrow match, Eton won again, though much more narrowly. A small, tough, ragged boy called Watts (I can't be sure who he was impersonating, possibly F. E. Covington) was bowling the last, critical over at the stumps chalked on the wall. I can see him now grimly summoning his field to the decisive effort: 'Nah then', he said, as he clutched the rubber ball, 'Nah then, 'Arrer!' He was a good performer, that boy Watts, and though that day was an Eton victory, he captained Farmer Road (under-12) when we won the Leyton Schools cup. In the final we were playing a side from a rather more affluent district of the borough. Nearly all of them wore white flannels. None of us did. Watts hit them all over the field. I would not swear that his shirt-tail was sticking out of a hole in his shorts, but it would not have been unusual. Later he captained Leyton Boys (under-15) at both football and cricket, and I am a little surprised, though of course one exaggerates the merits of one's own heroes, that I have heard no more of him. I am sure he had as much talent as many who really did play for 'Arrer.

Watts was also a sturdy partisan of Oxford in the days when the Boat Race battles came round. We could not reproduce rowing in the playground, but there were some famous fisticuffs. Everyone wore his light or dark blue favour. The object was to seize the favours of the enemy. It was preferable to be a Cambridge supporter then, since Cambridge won the Boat Race year after year, and I fear, still plunged in ignorance, I was one myself. But though numerically superior, we were far less confident in the playground than on the river, with Watts, so to speak, stroking Oxford. I ought not to give these names the orthodox spelling: it was *Orxford* and *Kimebridge*. Small boys – on the whole, it is an engaging thing about them – will take sides about anything. I remember the time the playground was riven by the great Brown Bread row. Two companies were marketing brown bread, with extensive advertising campaigns, Hovis and Daren. ''Ovis, 'Ovis!' cried one party, and 'Darren, Darren!' responded the other. I was a Daren man. I may not have been much good in the scraps, but I pulled my weight in the public relations department ('It's the *'olemeal* bread, see?'). I suppose we must have lost that battle, because it is a long time since I ate a slice of *Daren*.

After *The Story of the Tests* and *Ayres*, the next cricket book I remember reading was *Between the Wickets: An Anthology of Cricket*. It was edited by Eric Parker, and had been published by Philip Allan & Co. in 1926. Mine is a first edition. I have never come across a copy since, and I suppose there may never have been a second edition. It was a New Year's Eve, with a fog of the kind we used to call a 'London particular'. No one who did not experience them can imagine them. Dartmoor mists are nothing to them, though it is true that on Dartmoor you have the hazard of mire if, whether driving or on foot, you stray from the road. Father had been attending a ministers' fraternal at Stratford about five miles away; he had to walk home because there were no trams or buses, clinging to the railings most of the way; at some point he had paused in a second-hand bookshop, and noticing a book about cricket, had bought it for a few pence. Mother and I were worried about his late return, because there was a Watch Night Service to come, but late in the evening the key jangled, and there he was, my beloved father, emerging cheerfully though wearily from the yellow darkness. And he had brought me a cricket book.

I was then, I suppose, about 11, and less prone to tear the bindings off books when I became interested in them. The book is before me, in fair shape, today. It has the faults of an anthology: just when you are getting interested in something, it stops. But it also has the merit of an anthology, that it makes you want to read more. It demonstrated to me that there was a prairie of cricket writing which I had yet to tread. Most of the names in the index meant nothing to me then, but as I look at them today I can see how widely Parker had cast his net: William Barnes (the Dorset poet), E. E. Bowen (the Harrow songs man), Byron, Cardus (a shrewd pick, because he was then relatively unknown), Dickens, Pierce Egan, Felix, A. G. Gardiner, Thomas Hughes, R. A. Knox, Andrew Lang, John and Mary Russell Mitford, Pycroft, Francis Thompson, Wells. Lord! how lucky cricket has been in the people who have written about it. Parker included several excerpts of his own. He wrote a memoir of an interesting man, Hesketh Prichard, as well as *Playing Fields* to which I have referred. Later he wrote a history of cricket, in which he seems to have lost interest after he had dealt with the first hundred years, though the early chapters are very good. But for me, he is the editor of *Between the Wickets*, which father had paused to buy for me in the middle of a London particular.

Parker led me to John Nyren and Hambledon. It was some years before I read Nyren through, but Parker's numerous extracts laid the spell. Thus I grew up in the game with the companionship not only of Hobbs and Larwood, but Silver Billy and Lumpy. Hambledon played England on the blue carpet and beat them more often than not, even when the England innings was opened by Hobbs and Grace with Ranji at number three. Silver Billy Beldham scored freely against Barnes and Tate. He was represented on my carpet by a smock-frocked rustic, a relic of a toy farm. He really looked quite like the famous picture of Silver Billy in old age, though I cannot then have seen it.

I probably did not read *The Young Cricketer's Tutor* and *The Cricketers of my Time* right through until I went away to school. There was a tattered copy in the library. A copy of my own I did not possess until 1952, when the Sportsman's Book Club reprinted *The Hambledon Men*, a collection by E. V. Lucas which includes Nyren. After that Nyren was out of print for nearly a generation, until in 1974 Davis-Poynter produced a handsome new edition, with an introduction and notes by John Arlott. In his introduction, John says that after Nyren, 'nothing of comparable imaginative or literary standing was written on the game until Sir Neville Cardus's early reports'. This is not true, as Parker had taught me. However, it is probably true that there was no better writer between Nyren and Cardus of those who made cricket their principal subject (Cardus made his reputation as a cricket writer while still labouring up the ladder of music criticism). Nyren had no predecessors, and for a long time stood alone.

His book was published in 1833 when he was getting old, half a century from the prime of the cricketers he was describing. It is in two parts; *The Young Cricketer's Tutor* is little more than a guide to the game for boys, it has much to interest the antiquarian of cricket, but had he stopped there few others would have heard of him. The famous passages appear in the second part, *The Cricketers of My Time*. They had appeared as separate essays in a weekly periodical, *The Examiner*, and there had been requests that they should be reprinted (cheers for the requesters). So they were, on the face of it, a kind of appendix to the *Tutor*, despite the difference in style and quality between the two parts. It may be that the publishers used *The Cricketers* to fill out the Tutor, rather than the other way round.

The question of authorship has always been a vexed one. On the title page it is stated, 'The Whole Collected and Edited by Charles Cowden Clarke'. Cowden Clarke was a well-known literary figure of his time, an authority on Shakespeare (he and his daughter collaborated in the first Shakespearean concordance), a friend of Lamb, Hazlitt and Leigh Hunt. John Nyren was the son of a yeoman, Richard Nyren, who had been the first captain and secretary of the Hambledon Club. Richard placed, his son wrote, 'a full and just value upon the station he held in society, and he maintained it without insolence or assumption'. Nevertheless he was also the groundsman, and the landlord of the neighbouring 'Bat and Ball' inn, and in the second half of the eighteenth century the best of yeomen was some way from being a gentleman. So it has sometimes been assumed that when John Nyren came to write a book, he must have had the aid of a literary gentleman to a greater extent than is indicated, and that Cowden Clarke's 'editorship' amounts to full authorship.

However, in the long time that passed between the events he described and the publication of the book, John Nyren had risen in society, though his business career in calico printing failed when his factory was burnt down. He was musical, as the book shows. He played the violin, sang well and became a composer. He was choirmaster at St Mary, Moorfields, where Vincent Novello became organist. He would attend the musical evenings at Novello's home. Lamb was another frequenter of these occasions and, remembering them, quoted Isaac Watts:

> *I have been there, and still would go,*
> *'Twas like a little heaven below.*

Nyren uses the same couplet to describe the musical evenings long before at 'The Bat and Ball', when George Lear and Tom Sueter were singing glees together (both Nyren and Lamb make the same small misquotation, ' 'Twas' instead of ' 'Tis'). Cowden Clarke married one of Novello's daughters and lived for many years in the same household. No doubt in the intervals of the music on those evenings the notion of the book was born.

John Nyren's granddaughter told E. V. Lucas, a touch indignantly, that 'there is no doubt that John Nyren himself' wrote the book; but she was not a first-hand witness, and she also maintained, what is now known to be incorrect, that the Nyren family was descended from the Lords Nairne, who had forfeited their peerage because of their Jacobite activities. Cowden Clarke, in his preface to the second edition, after Nyren's death, says that the book was 'compiled from unconnected scraps and reminiscences during conversation'. He is not exactly an unprejudiced witness either, though he speaks warmly of Nyren, whom he calls the 'amiable Father' of the book. Also, it is said that Clarke never wrote anything so good at any other time – but while this seems likely, I cannot swear to it, because his output was very large and I have not read more than little bits of it. Perhaps it is significant that he was not in the ordinary way a writer who tempts you to go on reading him.

We must then put down the little miracle to a singularly fortunate collaboration, and I am pleased to record that my untutored taste recognised it at once as a masterpiece. Reading it again, especially the most famous passage, I am reminded of the radio programme, 'Country Magazine', which ran for many years at Sunday lunchtime. Ralph Wightman introduced it, and I was one of its many producers. The programme at least in its earlier days was broadcast live, with country people reading from scripts, under Ralph's benevolent guidance. The scripts were prepared well beforehand by assiduous producers and stenographers, from conversations with those who were to take part. It was a matter of skill to give them scripts which reflected their natural style of speaking, expressed their feelings and were not too difficult to read. It was a programme of merit, but had some hilarious moments. One old gentleman ascribed the long life he had led to hard work. 'If you had your time over again', asked Ralph, 'would you work so hard?' 'No', said the old man, struggling with his script, 'I would not work so hard, I would do more scheming like they do today, laughter.' It was a taxing moment for Ralph as he produced his usual sympathetic laugh.

A more frequent hazard was that because they knew that they were talking 'for a programme', the performers, even in the preliminary discussions, tended to risk the unfamiliar phrase, the posh phrase. Consider this from Nyren, which might easily have come from a nineteenth-century 'Country Magazine' script:

> Oh! it was a heart-stirring sight to witness the multitude forming a complete and dense circle round that noble green. Half the county would be present, and all their hearts with us – little Hambledon, pitted against all England, was a proud thought for the Hampshire men . . . And then, what stuff they had to drink! Punch! not your modern cat-lap punch, punch be-devilled; but good, unsophisticated John Bull stuff – stark! – that would stand on end – punch that would make a cat speak! Sixpence a bottle! We had not sixty millions of interest to pay in those days!

I have only shortened it a little, taking out what I deem to be a Clarkism or two. I can hear John Nyren saying it – not all at once, but with the aid of a good stenographer putting it together. The brief single words and phrases: Punch! Stark! Sixpence a Bottle! ring true, and even the sarcastic aside, 'We had not sixty millions of interest to pay.' In such passages Cowden Clarke was doing no more than was achieved by Ralph Wightman and his staff in 'Country Magazine'. The voice is authentic.

Here, for comparison, is a twentieth-century account of village cricket, which I take from *Country Magazine: The Book of the BBC Programme*, edited by Francis Dillon, published by Odhams Press about 1950. After a rather pretentious introduction, for which I fear Francis Dillon must have been responsible – 'On the village green the last of the squires and the first of the new aristocrats meet . . .' – Cowden Clarke gives way to Nyren, represented in this case by Eric Eaton of the Stonehouse club, Gloucestershire.

Our pavilion is a glorified cart-shed, big enough to hold one cart. It may sound a bit comical, but we can play, I'll tell you that. We only lost three matches out of eighteen last season and have won eight out of nine this . . . We get a big crowd watching too. There's a great many toffs living round the village and on Sundays you can see them walking up the road with their deck-chairs under their arms. But I don't think I've ever seen anyone go to sleep at one of our matches. You see, it's not like county cricket, it's much faster and there's too much to laugh at. We've got one man whose whites are specially well looked after, snow-white everything, shirt and trousers always perfectly laundered, but he will insist on coming out with his black braces and black boots on top of it all. Of course they all laugh, but they don't laugh when he starts to bat, believe me . . .

I think I pretty near live for cricket. You see, it's not like football, there's more to it than just the game. The finest sight I know is of whites on a good field, especially where we are, with the hills flowing away up behind them and the trees and grass and everything so green and everybody lazing around and easy.

Nyren's book did give us a distorted picture of early cricket history. The importance of Hambledon was exaggerated simply because the book was so good. Other places with equal claims to fame had no comparable spokesman. John Arlott, honest Hampshireman, accepted this in his introduction to the new edition. We no longer use of Hambledon the phrase 'the cradle of cricket'. Yet it remains remarkable that at a critical stage in the development of the game, this out-of-the-way village had so much influence, and there is no obvious explanation save Hampshire enterprise and Hampshire skill. However much of the book Nyren wrote, and however much Clarke wrote, they could not have done it without their material.

At the end, Nyren chooses his best Hambledon eleven, inventing a happy precedent for the familiar game. His selection is slightly unexpected since he has not mentioned two of the names before, but he concludes proudly: 'No eleven in England could have had any chance with these men, and I think they might have beaten any two-and-twenty.' And the Reverend James Mitford echoed him in his review of the book in *The Gentleman's Magazine*:

> Troy has fallen, and Thebes is a ruin. The pride of Athens is decayed, and Rome is crumbling to the dust. The philosophy of Bacon is wearing out; and the victories of Marlborough have been overshadowed by fresher laurels. All is vanity but CRICKET; all is sinking in oblivion but you. Greatest of all elevens, fare ye well!

It is absurd even as hyperbole: but I caught something of his feelings when I first read Nyren; and still do as I look back upon, for instance, 'those anointed clod-stumpers', the Walkers, and the dignified exchange of gifts between the Duke of Dorset and John Small, and the tale of Noah Mann, swarthy as a gipsy, who would stoop to pick up handkerchiefs from the ground as he galloped his horse, and who died from falling drunkenly upon an inn fire, and won a match for Hambledon against England when ten were needed, furious at being put in last, while Sir Horace Mann (no relation) was walking about outside the ground cutting down the daisies with his stick, 'the old farmers leaning forward on their tall old staves, and the whole multitude perfectly still . . .'

My next, and most significant experience in cricket reading I can date precisely. It was my introduction to Cardus. When Cardus died in 1975 a memorial service was held for him in St Paul's, Covent Garden. The Royal Philharmonic Orchestra, conducted by James Loughran of the Hallé, gave us Elgar and Mozart, and Clifford Curzon played. Wendy Hiller and Flora Robson read poems. Much to my surprise, I was asked to give the address. I have never been more nervous about anything in my life. But *Wisden* thought it worth reproducing, and I take the liberty of reproducing it again (more or less: a man can never vouch for every word he has spoken on such occasions), not because I think it was all that good, but because I was so proud to have been asked. It also fits in

well at this point of the book, because it explains how I first came
to read Cardus.

Since we are in a church, I thought it proper that we should have
a text. Hear then these words from the prophet Blake (I am not
sure whether Blake was one of Sir Neville's favourites, though
he has recalled how enthusiastically he would join in 'Jeru-
salem' in his days with the Ancoats Brotherhood). Blake wrote,
in *Auguries of Innocence*,

> *Joy and woe are woven fine,*
> *A clothing for the soul divine;*
> *Under every grief and pine*
> *Runs a thread of silken twine.*

On such an occasion as this, joy and woe are inseparable
companions: thanksgiving for such a life, sadness that it has
ended. But more than that: it was the mingling of joy and woe
that made Sir Neville such a writer – the sensitivity to the human
condition, not least his own; the ability to observe it, and to
communicate what he saw, with detachment and yet with
passion. His books are full of humour: rich comedy, sometimes
almost slapstick, and yet he keeps us hovering between tears
and laughter. For always he is conscious, and makes us
conscious, of the fragility of happiness, of the passing of time.
He loved the good moments all the more avidly because he
knew they were fleeting.

There is no need to recite his achievement. His autobiographical books, the crown of his life's work, have done that
already. His early cricket books gave him a reputation for 'fancy'
writing. The words 'lyrical', 'rhapsodical', were sometimes
applied to him, usually by people who would not know a lyric
from a rhapsody. These terms were still jostled about long after
they had any possible justification. His mature prose was
marked by clarity, balance, and indeed restraint, though he
never shrank from emotion or from beauty. Perhaps George
Orwell was as good a writer of prose; or you may think of
P. G. Wodehouse, or Bernard Darwin – everyone has his own
favourites – but in this century it is not easy to think of many
more in the same class.

I remember clearly how I was introduced to Cardus's writing.
It was in August, 1935. We were on holiday in Cornwall, at St

Ives, and my father was buying me a book, because of some small family service I had done. I said I would like a cricket book, and the choice narrowed to two: a book of reminiscences attributed to Hendren, I think it was, and *Good Days* by Neville Cardus. I doubt if I had heard of Cardus then, because it was difficult to get *The Manchester Guardian* in the south of England. I was inclined to Hendren, but father was inclined to Cardus. Father won. We bought *Good Days*. Father read it before I did, though I have more than made up for it since. Most of us, perhaps half a dozen times in our lives, read books – not always famous books – which change us, change our thinking, books which open doors, revelatory books. That was one of mine. It was the essay on Emmott Robinson that did it – do you remember it? – when Cardus imagined that 'the Lord one day gathered together a heap of Yorkshire clay, and breathed into it, and said "Emmott Robinson, go on and bowl at the pavilion end for Yorkshire." ' And then the next bit, about how Emmott's trousers were always on the point of falling down, and he would remember to grab them just in time.

All cricket writers of the last half century have been influenced by Cardus, whether they admit it or not, whether they have wished to be or not, whether they have tried to copy him or tried to avoid copying him. He was not a model, any more than Macaulay, say, was a model for the aspiring historian. But just as Macaulay changed the course of the writing of history, Cardus changed the course of the writing of cricket. He showed what could be done. He dignified and illumined the craft.

It was, it occurs to me, fortunate for cricket that Bradman and Cardus existed at the same time: fortunate for them, too, since the best of batsmen was recorded by the best of critics. Each was worthy of the other.

In the music of Sir Neville's time, at least in English music, there was never one figure quite so dominant as Bradman. Elgar, Delius and Beecham were, he wrote, 'the three most original spirits known in English music since Purcell, if we leave out Sullivan'. He said it with a shadow of a wink, as if to say, 'and take it out of that'. You remember how he described Delius, when he met him in what now seem the improbable surroundings of the Langham Hotel: 'His attendant carried him into the sitting-room of his suite and flopped him down on a couch, where he fell about like a rag doll until he was arranged into a semblance of human shape. There was nothing pitiable in him, nothing inviting sympathy in this wreck of a physique. He was wrapped in a monk-like gown, and his face was strong and disdainful, every line on it grown by intrepid living.' There is a picture for you, there is a piece of prose for you.

As for Sir Thomas Beecham, he is always bursting out of Cardus's pages and making his own way. It was with some difficulty that Cardus stopped his splendid Aunt Beatrice from conquering his first autobiographical book. He never quite stopped Beecham, any more than Shakespeare ever stopped Falstaff taking charge of Henry the Fourth.

Perhaps the most remarkable episode in the life of Cardus, and one to which we should refer here, was his conversion. I think the word is properly used: I mean his conversion to music. It was achieved by one of the minor saints: Edward German. He was watching a production of a light opera, *Tom Jones*, at the Prince's Theatre, Manchester. He had gone there because he was reading Henry Fielding, but, he says, 'the music of Edward German got past my ears and entered into my mind behind my back'. Only twenty months after that first experience, he was listening to the first performance of Elgar's Symphony in A flat, and wondering, with the other musicians in the audience, how Elgar was going to cope with such a long first subject.

He used to say that he was baffled that it should have been Edward German who first revealed the light: yet he should not have been. It was all of a piece of the man and his thought. When Beecham and MacLaren, and Bradman and Ranjitsinhji, and Elgar and Delius, came within the experience of Cardus, he rose to them and did them justice – but he was capable of being moved, such was his sense of humanity, by men who were no more than good county bowlers, Emmott Robinson and Edward German.

'Joy and woe are woven fine'. They are not alien, they are complementary, 'A clothing for the soul divine.' And in another part of that poem, Blake says

> *It is right it should be so,*
> *Man was made for joy and woe,*
> *And when this we rightly know,*
> *Safely through the world we go.*

I am not sure whether Sir Neville would approve of that as an epitaph: but he is probably too busy to bother just now, arguing with Bernard Shaw.

In 1938 I read the second edition newly published of *A History of Cricket* by H. S. Altham and E. W. Swanton. It was given to me for my fifteenth birthday and is still with me. So by then, with my first *Wisden*, I had acquired at least the beginnings of a sound cricketing library. Of other early books, I still possess *Cricket in Firelight*, by Richard Binns (Selwyn & Blount, 1935). That appealed to me very much, partly because Binns was a Yorkshireman, and had, when a boy, seen Yorkshire bowl out the 1902 Australians for twenty-three. I am sorry he did not so far as I know publish any more about cricket, for he was a good writer. I also have *For England and Yorkshire* by Herbert Sutcliffe, which I read soon after it came out (Edward Arnold & Co., 1935). When I went away to school I found a few cricketing books in the library, mostly instructional, but I enjoyed *Cricket Memories* by 'Country Vicar'.

'Country Vicar' was the pseudonym of the Reverend R. L. Hodgson, who played for Lincolnshire in his youth, and for many years held a living at South Baddesley in Hampshire. He wrote for *The Cricketer* in every issue for more than twenty years, these articles forming the foundation of his books. E. W. Swanton has written that 'my suspicious mind suggests that part of the charm for Plum [Warner was then editor] of this ceaseless cascade of words was that they were either cheap or even written "for love" '. I dare say this was true, but I will put in a word for 'Country Vicar'. I was much taken by *Cricket Memories*, and appreciated the later books. I still often read a chapter or two. I suppose my affection for him, in youth, derived partly from the fact that he too was a Yorkshireman, and not only that, a Cambridge man, so that we had deeply shared sympathies. Jim says of him that he wrote 'agreeable nostalgic stuff', but I would put him a shade higher than that.

Herbert Sutcliffe's book contained, in a preface by Lord Hawke, the statement that it had 'the outstanding distinction of having been written, every word of it, by himself'. I did not take much notice of this at the time. Youthful innocent, I still assumed that the writer of a book was the man whose name appeared on the cover. But I now realise that Sutcliffe was setting a precedent for a cricket professional in this respect, as he did in several others. Indeed not only for professionals. Hawke's own reminiscences appear to have been largely put together by Sir Home Gordon. Apart from the suggestion by Sir Home (not always a reliable witness) the stylistic evidence points that way. I do not know that I have ever read a better *authentic* book by a cricketer than *For England and Yorkshire*, until Michael Brearley came along.

Not that I wish to be unkind to Hawke or Sir Home. Hawke's book, which I did not read until much later, contains some memorable passages. My copy came to a sad end. I lent it to a friend, whose house shortly afterwards caught fire. The books which the fire did not spoil the hoses did. However, I still have a copy of *Herbert Farjeon's Cricket Bag* (Macdonald, 1946) which contains the following paragraph. Under the heading 'Gems from Lord Hawke', he has this to say of the book:

> Quite the best sentence is this one about Rhodes: 'The presentation of his portrait to me last year was the crowning tribute to his wonderful career.' But other passages run it close, and every page is worth reading, no matter whether Hawke is proclaiming 'I believe I have done more than anyone else to raise the standard and self-respect of the splendid-paid section of first-class cricketers', or whether, descanting on the felicity of his married life, he remarks, 'I think I can safely say I have drawn a prize in the matrimonial lottery. Even in golf my wife and I are well-matched.'

Those few sentences tell you most you need to know about Hawke, and about Gordon, whose cramped style is unmistakable. He always had trouble with hyphens. Swanton wrote a very amusing and not altogether unsympathetic sketch of him in *Follow On* (Collins, 1977). Gordon was another who gave his services without charge to *The Cricketer*. There were times when they wondered whether it was worth it. He is reported to have said to Warner, who once offered a mild rebuke, 'My dear Plum, Neville Cardus has his style, I have mine' – indisputably true. All the same I value his book, *Background of Cricket*, published in 1939. Warner had given it a stiff review in *The Cricketer*, of which I remember the phrase 'parts of it should never have been written'. It sounded an interesting, slightly malicious, gossipy book, and so it proved. I have it by me now, and much of the gossipy bits have long been confirmed by more illustrious sources. I have known E.W.S. refer to it (not in print, needless to say) as 'Backside of Cricket', which is not a bad description, and after all, in the immortal line of the poet Vaughan, 'How brave a prospect is a bright backside!'

I have so far only mentioned *A History of Cricket* in passing. There have only been three major histories of the game, though others have been published with that title, several with merit (I enjoyed T.E.B.'s, though it might have been more appropriately entitled 'A History of Bailey'). There was Parker, unsurpassed on the early days, Bowen, whose scope was the widest, since he covered the whole world, and Altham and Swanton. Altham was responsible for the original, which took us up to 1926 or so, Swanton for the subsequent revisions. It remains the best-written and most authoritative of the three. My first 1938 edition has long lost its covers through avid reading in youth and constant reference since, but no book on my cricket shelves do I value more.

I knew H. S. Altham only slightly, though sufficiently to appreciate his vast cricketing knowledge and genial wisdom. Jim, as he has always been called, has become over the years a warm friend: the most cherished I have made in cricket writing, apart from the cricket correspondent of *The Times*, John Woodcock (I am not counting Arlott as a cricket writer for present purposes, and will come to him later). In 1972 Jim published his autobiography, *Sort of A Cricket Person*. It has since been pleasingly supplemented, and I dare say will be again, but that book contains the essential Swanton.

The most important thing to remember about Jim is that he is a Christian. His religious experience was deepened by his grim years as a prisoner of the Japanese. One of the best broadcasts he ever made was in a programme called 'Christian Forum', in which I took the chair. When asked to take part, he was reluctant, unsure whether he should. 'There are holes in my Christianity', he explained, in a gracious phrase which has always stayed in my mind. He is a High Churchman, and I have heard him ask Richard Maddock, on a Saturday at a Birmingham or Nottingham Test, for advice as to which church he should attend next day to be sure of 'sound catholic doctrine'. Richard Maddock was the radio producer in charge of all the Tests in the Midlands for more than twenty years, and is a devout churchman himself, the brother of a bishop.

Jim has been often teased about his pomposity. In the middle of a Test match at Lord's, which happened to coincide with a papal election, great bursts of black smoke suddenly emerged from the tall chimneys that used to stand behind the Tavern at Lord's. 'Lord', said Brian Johnstone, who was commentating at the time, 'they've elected Swanton Pope.' I suppose it is possible that Jim, who came to a senior position in cricket writing very young in life, did tend to assert himself too much, at times. 'Come in quick', St Peter is supposed to have said to a psychiatrist at the pearly gates, in one version of an old story, and 'Having trouble with God thinks he's Jim Swanton'. But Jim knew about these jokes and did not resent them: indeed he relished them. This is another aspect of his Christian character. A third is that, when all the South African arguments were at their height, he took the side of Edward Boyle and David Sheppard, and stood out against the 1970 tour. As Jim is instinctively a Tory (and remains so in most respects) this must have been, whatever your own views, an immensely courageous thing for him to do. He gave affront to many old friends, which gave him real pain. But he had decided where his duty lay.

When I reviewed *Sort of A Cricket Person*, I concluded with a quotation from Addison:

> *In all thy Humours, whether grave or mellow,*
> *Thour't such a touchy, testy, pleasant Fellow;*
> *Hast so much Wit, and Mirth, and Spleen about thee,*
> *There is no living with thee, nor without thee.*

Jim has been the Addison of cricket writers. Cardus, you might say, the Hazlitt. To pursue the rather contrived analogy, Nyren/ Cowden Clarke was the Herodotus, Altham the Thucydides.

Robertson-Glasgow was, I suppose, the Wodehouse. Do not think this is a slur upon him, because Wodehouse is one of the best English writers of the twentieth century. But rather strangely I read very little of Robertson-Glasgow in my earlier years, and I never met him.

This chapter, however, gives you some account of the reading that helped to make my cricket background.

XI
Heroes

'You ask me for a charm against disease –
Not of the body (you can bow to that),
But of the spirit, which you tremble at,
Lest it should dull your fine-wrought sympathies
With vigorous human life, and slowly freeze
The sinews of your mind, till they grow dumb
As the dead limbs they live with, and become
Useless for all high purposes like these.
What is my counsel?
                                    Choose a hero'.
Edward Cracoft Lefroy, 'Sonnet to an Invalid'

'Les temps heroiques sont passes'
Gambetta

My first cricketing Hero was Sutcliffe, my last was Hutton. In between, Leyland and Verity had qualified for the capital H. All Yorkshiremen, you notice. There were several small-h heroes, such as O'Connor and Donnelly, but for me hero-worship began with Sutcliffe and ended with Hutton. This does not mean that there have been no heroes since Hutton. It simply means that I lost my capacity for worshipping them. More than that: I gradually lost my capacity for partisanship. When Hutton was made England's first professional captain in 1952, when he won the Ashes in 1953, and retained them in Australia in 1954–55, I felt that a chapter in my life had been concluded. So possibly did Hutton, who retired soon afterwards. In the next few years I continued to enjoy cricket, and still often do: but the agony and the ecstasy had gone with the departure of the last hero.

I am rather ashamed in fact that they persisted so long. I remained, in cricketing enthusiasms, a small boy until I was 30. I suppose there is no real harm in this, but it does not make for good judgment, and by then I was reporting the game professionally, even if only occasionally. But it was not deliberately or consciously that I shed the mantle of partisanship. It just fell away. I noticed that I did not greatly care any more who won a match. I would sometimes wish that the clock would hurry along to half-past six. I do not mean that I lost interest in cricket, but I viewed it with more detachment, and in consequence reported it much better.

F. W. Boreham, a great Australian preacher, whose published sermons (more like brief essays) still read well, tells of re-reading some of his earlier efforts. He was surprised and rather dismayed by how many of his paragraphs began with 'O!'. 'O, my friends, could I but tell you . . .' 'O, sisters and brethren, believe me . . .' 'O, to have been with the Lord that day . . .' and so on. And he realised that this was an immature style; yet recognised a longing for those early days when his instinctive response to some new revelation of the truth was to cry 'O!' He wishes that he could utter it with the same happy conviction in his old age as he had done in his youth. He had become much more deeply informed in the Christian faith, but the touches of spontaneous joy had gone.

Hutton was the last batsman who drew from me the uncritical, awed, joyful 'O!' Of the three Yorkshire cricketers who have scored a hundred centuries, I think Hutton was technically the best, Boycott second and Sutcliffe third: but Sutcliffe would always have been the one to choose to score a hundred for your life. He had the temperament for it. The big occasion brought out the best in him. In 1939, Warner wrote in *The Cricketer*, when Sutcliffe had scored four consecutive centuries, that if England had to play a match upon which the destiny of the nation depended, he would choose Sutcliffe as number one. This seemed to me at the time, and still does, a half-hearted apology for leaving him out of the 1936–7 side to Australia, and preferring Edrich in 1938.

Sutcliffe was not so handsome a stroke player as Hammond, nor so prolific in runs as Hobbs, though his average of sixty-six is still the highest recorded in Test matches against Australia. This is to exclude Paynter, who only played in seven Australian Tests against Sutcliffe's twenty-seven. An interrogator once pointed out to Paynter that his average of 83 owed much to the 216 not out he made at Trent Bridge in 1938, when he went in at 244 for 3. 'Oh ay', said Paynter, 'ay, it were mostly due to that 216.' He paused, and added, 'Still, they had to be made, tha knows.' Eddie Paynter was a lovely, tough little Lancastrian, a left-hander, who would have played more often for England had he not coincided with Leyland.

Sutcliffe played Test cricket from 1924, when he was chosen as Hobbs's partner at home against South Africa, and accompanied him to Australia the following winter, until 1935, when after the second Test against South Africa he was injured. Nobody imagined that his departure from the side would be more than temporary, but he never played for England again. Of the 1936 to 1937 tour in Australia, when Verity had to open the innings in a Test because the supposed batsmen were not up to it, Swanton writes: 'How the captain must have sighed for Sutcliffe – and how Sutcliffe, as he listened-in at his native Pudsey, must have longed to be there! Forty-two did indeed seem an early age at which to relegate to the shelf the most successful of all English batsmen against Australia.'

Sutcliffe played his last match for Yorkshire in 1939, so his first-class career exactly spanned the interwar years. In the first war he had been a lieutenant; in the second he was a major. He was always officer material. In his later life I met him on a number of occasions. My awe of him and admiration of him remained undimmed even during a Scarborough Festival when he was president, and I the representative of *The Times*. On all the posh occasions he politely introduced me as 'My friend, Alan Thomson.' Kind acquaintances sought to put him right, but he ignored them. His view was that my name must be Thomson, since he had taken the trouble to remember it.

This was the same Sutcliffe of whom Cardus wrote, the Sutcliffe who, after a fierce hit on the thigh or shin, waved back the sympathising fieldsmen, as if to say 'We Sutcliffes do not feel pain.' It was the same Sutcliffe who, after he had played a ball into his stumps, quite hard, and the bails did not fall, and someone said 'Close shave, Herbert', replied 'I haven't the least idea what you are talking about', and took guard, brow unfurrowed, for the next ball, the hair as always immaculate. He had scored 40 against Australia that day, but he had scored 194 by the time he was out. He had decreed that he was destined for a century, just as he decreed many years later that my name was Thomson.

His batting, as I remember, and as most judges confirm, was mostly a square drive, a cover drive and a furious hook. The hook sometimes got him out, caught in the deep – the Australians often bowled for the stroke, now and then successfully – but it brought him thousands of runs. He never flinched from the fast bowlers, and he played against two of the fastest, MacDonald (who moved from Australia to Lancashire) and Larwood. Nottinghamshire and Yorkshire would employ a body-line field against each other in the early 1930s, and Sutcliffe seems rather to have enjoyed it. He would hook MacDonald and Larwood with aplomb, and with Eau-de-Cologne under his armpits. Oh, he was a dandy cricketer! Yorkshiremen of a different mould, such as Robinson or Macaulay, disapproved of the fancy touches, but could not bring themselves to disapprove of the batsman.

Sutcliffe was too uncertain against leg-spin to be put in the very highest class of batsmen. He would have enjoyed himself in the last decade, now that leg-spin has vanished from the English scene. Yet he did not do too badly against Grimmett and O'Reilly. Indeed, I think this is a point where a few figures are permissible, since the feeling persists that he was a lucky batsman, and a bit of a scratcher whenever the ball turned from leg. This was, generously, suggested by Ray Robinson, one of the best Australian writers on the game, in his book *Between Wickets*:

> Each Australian leg-break bowler who met Sutcliffe for the first time, and saw him feeling for the ball, smiled inwardly at the prospect of an early snicked catch and wondered how a batsman with such a rudimentary flaw in his technique could have won his way into a Test team. Four hours or so later they would still be wondering – and Sutcliffe would be majestically acknowledging the crowd's applause for his hundred.

Sutcliffe batted in six rubbers against Australia, and in no series was his average less than fifty. In 1924–5 the Australian bowlers included Mailey and (for the last Test) Grimmett. In 1926 the same two were there, and Macartney, though not the bowler he had been, was an accurate slow-medium left-hander, who could also make the ball leave the bat. In 1928–9 there was Grimmett again, with Ironmonger, slow left-hand, in support. Ironmonger was a formidable bowler, who took seventy-four wickets at an average of under eighteen, in fourteen Tests, but never toured, because, it was said, English umpires would never have passed his action. Grimmett's best year in England was 1930, and there was also Hornibrook, slow left-hand, who took seven for ninety-two in the second innings of the decisive final Test. In 1932–3 Grimmett was joined by O'Reilly as well as Ironmonger, and in 1934 it was Grimmett and O'Reilly again, with useful leg-spin support from

Chipperfield. So if Sutcliffe persisted in scoring runs, it was not because there was any lack of bowlers turning the ball from the leg to challenge him. Ray Robinson points out that of his forty-one dismissals against Australia, Sutcliffe was twenty-five times out to leg-spin, but that cannot have been disproportionate to the number of overs bowled at him; and they all had to pay for it.

Still, statistics are not really in place when considering a hero. Of his two famous, Ashes-winning partnerships with Hobbs at the Oval in 1926 and at Melbourne in 1929, I have written elsewhere, and so come to think of it has just about everyone else who has written about cricket at all. They showed the man at his best, all tenacity, calm amid the whirlwinds. 'I play each ball on its merits', he said. 'If I am beaten all ends up, and get away with it, I have forgotten about it as soon as the bowler starts his run for the next delivery. Remember that the bowler can deliver only one ball at a time.' This, agreed Ray Robinson ruefully, is 'an unanswerable piece of philosophy': though it was not exactly original. It was, I think, W.G. who had first said 'There is no crisis in cricket. Only the next ball.'

It was a stupid waste that Herbert Sutcliffe – though the idea was proposed – never became captain of Yorkshire. Had he done so, he would almost certainly have become captain of England, and made the pattern of cricket in the 1930s and thereafter smoother. But that too is another long and complicated story. When I heard that he was dead, even though he had reached 83, I felt real sadness. The heroes of boyhood are not lightly lost, and I mourned him as deeply as every other Thomson in the land.

Maurice Leyland came into the Yorkshire side some years after Sutcliffe. He was much more a Yorkshire boy's image of what a Yorkshire cricketer should be. He was not so good a batsman, but he shared the quality of rising to the big occasion, and was never more dangerous than in a Test match. Distrusting figures though I do, these give you the clue to Leyland. In his first-class career, which lasted from 1920 to 1948 (though essentially it was from 1922 to 1946) he scored 33,659 runs at an average of 40.50. Now that was pretty good, though lesser batsmen have done comparably. John Langridge, for instance, in a career which went from 1928 to 1955, scored more runs, though his average was three points lower; and John Langridge never played for England. Hardinge of Kent scored almost as many runs as Leyland, playing from 1902 to 1933, again with an average a few down. Hardinge played for England only once. Cricketers have shorter careers and play less innings nowadays, but you would not think from his county figures that Leyland was a better bat than, say, Martin Young of Gloucestershire or Alan Ormrod of Worcestershire, who came later. Sound stuff, yes, but nothing to startle. However, when you look at his average in *Test* cricket, you find that it has gone up to forty-six; and when you look at his average against *Australia*, and you must remember that in his time the Australian matches dominated over all, you find it has gone up to fifty-six. He scored eighty centuries in first-class cricket, and seven of them were against Australia. He was always at his best when the opposition was at its toughest. He used to look forward to batting against Bill O'Reilly, and he was the only English batsman of his time who did.

When Leyland began with Yorkshire they thought him a bit too dashing. He was a left-hander who liked to cut. They also wondered whether he might make a better bowler, also left-handed, slow, a possible successor to Rhodes. But his batting was the first to blossom. In 1923, he scored a thousand runs, the first of seventeen consecutive seasons when he did so (two thousand in 1933, and again in 1934). When the 1928–9 side to Australia was announced, Leyland was in it. There was a huge row about this. I was just old enough, living in Ilkley as I was, 5 years old, to remember it. The Ilkley men, solemnly lighting their pipes for the usual cricket chat after Sunday morning chapel, were of course strongly in favour, but I understood that the abominated southerners were kicking up a fuss. 'Leyland' became a kind of password among Yorkshire boys. I was at the Grove School, one of those described as 'for girls and little boys', run by the admirable Miss Wilkinson. We little boys used to mutter to each other the magic name as a talisman. The girls, mostly older and posher (they were *never* sent to stand in a corner) would look perplexed. Then there came a girl called Eileen, about my own age, and I became rather fond of her. Now I come to think of it, I was several times lucky with Eileens. She was not at all put off by our murmurs of 'Leyland', and replied swiftly with 'Maurice'. I knew at once she was a girl in a thousand. I must have been seven years or so older, living in London by then, travelling back to the north to visit relations, when the train paused for a while at Leyland. I leant out of the window and gave it three cheers. Later I discovered that it was in Lancashire which was a pity. Later still the name came to have not

142 of Growing Up With Cricket

altogether happy industrial implications. But the cheers were well meant and heartfelt.

But I must go back to the 1928–9 side chosen for Australia. What caused the rumpus was that another left-hander, the famous Woolley, had been left out, news hardly believed and badly received in Kent. Woolley scored over 3000 runs in 1928, and had played in every match in every rubber against Australia since 1911. He was, it was firmly thought by everyone south of the Trent, much the greatest and most elegant left-handed batsman in the world; and to think he was left out in favour of an uncouth Yorkshireman with no style at all to speak of . . .

I look back on this argument, the first cricketing argument in which I am conscious of having taken sides, and realise that whatever we thought in Ilkley and whatever they thought down in Kent, the real choice must have been between Woolley and Mead, of Hampshire. Mead was also a left-hander, who scored 3000 runs that season, and had toured Australia with Woolley in 1911–12. He was stodgy compared with Woolley or Leyland, but was judged, with his cautious technique, to be a better bet, if not a better bat than Woolley, on Australian pitches in time-unlimited Tests. Warner, who was on the selection committee, says that 'what eventually weighted the scales against "The Pride of Kent" was the essential need of an active outfield like Leyland', and this was undoubtedly true, for this side, for all its batting virtuosity, was an oldish one. It does not, however, quite answer the criticism that Woolley aged 41 was a likelier fielder than Mead, just two months older. A correspondent of Warner's described Mead as 'a leaden-footed cart-horse', and G. J. V. Weigall, a friend of Warner's, called Leyland not for the last time 'a cross-batted village-greener'.

Well, it did not turn out to matter much, because England, whose batting order usually began Hobbs, Sutcliffe, Hammond, Jardine, Hendren – surely as good an opening five as we have ever had – won the rubber by a massive weight of runs. Mead played in the first Test, when he scored eight and seventy-three. Leyland was brought in for the last, the only one that Australia won, given a game only because Sutcliffe and Chapman were unfit. He did very well, scoring 137 and 53.

After this performance, it was thought that he would be one of the leading English batsmen when Australia came here in 1930. This was the first year I began to pay some attention to the Test scores, and of course after all those conversations outside Ilkley

Baptist Chapel, I was a Leyland man. He was in good form that season, but was not chosen until the third Test (Woolley had played in the first two) and it was a disappointing series for him. He scored forty-four and one not out in the third, thirty-five in the fourth, three and twenty-eight in the fifth. The first time I could claim to have seen him bat was at the cinema, and it was the first time I had been taken to the cinema. I was completely bemused and baffled by the whole thing, unable to take it in. The main film, I think, was *The Gold Rush* – certainly it was an early Chaplin. The posters outside announced that there would also be film of the fifth Test match, which was why I looked forward to going. Leyland was come and gone in a flash. I had not even realised it was Leyland. 'See that?', said my father by my side, 'Leyland bowled for three.' However, I was to be lucky enough to see a good deal more of Leyland later on.

Woolley, in his Tests that season, had scored nought, five, forty-one and twenty-eight, so Leyland had slightly the better of it when you worked the averages out, but still he had not done enough to please the Yorkshiremen, and, even more important we felt in our mean northern way, displease the Kentishmen. There was considerable doubt whether he should be chosen for Jardine's tour of Australia, but a good run of scores in the latter part of the 1932 season secured his place. He played in all five Tests, averaging thirty-four. At Adelaide he scored eighty-three, after England had lost four wickets for thirty. This was one of many instances when he showed his value in a crisis. The circumstances in which a batsman makes his runs are often a better guide to his abilities than their actual number. He began and ended the series with nought, but on both occasions England were in a strong position. I listened each morning to the broadcasts on the BBC from Australia – five-minute live reports by Alan Kippax. He was very good at the job. Radio Luxembourg, or Radio Normandy, or someone like that were doing bogus commentaries, but I had the sense to realise that they were frauds, and after a few experiments stuck to Kippax. He usually approved of Leyland. He was a generous Australian commentator in a difficult series, and it may not just be the haze of distance which makes me think of him as the best at the early-waking five-minuter until Jim Swanton came along, many years later.

Leyland's great year against Australia was 1934: three centuries, all of them in times of trouble. Sutcliffe did not score a Test century that season, and though he finished with an average of just over fifty, it was to Leyland that the boy's heart turned. In 1936–7 Leyland scored two more in Australia, including what many consider his best innings, 126 in the first Test after England had lost 3 for 20. In 1938 he did not play until the last Test, left out – as Tom Webster put it – 'through a bad shoulder and bad selection'. He then scored 187 in the record-breaking second-wicket part-nership with Hutton. He carried on for a season after the war, and though he was by then, in the old phrase, batting from memory, he had the satisfaction of thwarting Lancashire when they looked like winning.

You might think from his reputation as a life-saver, an illustra-tion of what Jardine used to call 'concrete in the middle of the order', that Leyland was a dour batsman. Nothing of the kind. He usually scored quickly, even in Tests, and often lost his wicket through readiness to take risks. When I saw him bat this genial anxiety to get a move on sometimes irritated me. He was only careless when there was nothing much at stake – but, whatever the state of the match, there *was* something at stake for me, because I was watching him. On the other hand, I suppose that if he had played more cautiously, he would not have stamped himself so firmly into my memory. If he feared fast bowling, you would never have guessed it (his remark has often been quoted, 'None of us likes it, but not all of us lets on'). He did not have any of the great Australian fast bowlers with whom to contend, but scored plenty of runs in domestic cricket against Larwood, Voce and Farnes. The principal Australian menace in his best years was O'Reilly, who bowled medium-paced leg-spin. He played O'Reilly better than any other English batsman, even Hammond, partly of course because he was left-handed. In the Oval Test of 1938, when England batted first, Edrich was soon out. Leyland came in at number three, higher than expected. When he saw who was arriving, O'Reilly clasped his head and said, 'Oh, it's that bloody Yorkshireman again.' So it has been reported, and though I was not near enough to hear the language, I can vouch for the clasping of the head.

His shade would not forgive me if I said nothing more of his bowling. He took 466 wickets at an average of under 30, but with the competition in the Yorkshire side so severe he was gradually reduced to a partnership-breaker, bowling out of the back of the hand as often as not. I once heard him claim that he originated or was the cause of origin of the term 'Chinaman', the slow left-hander's googly. When Yorkshire were stuck and the opposing partnership was growing too formidable, someone would say, 'Put on Maurice to bowl some of those Chinese things.' In 1938, a dry summer which did not give the orthodox spinners many bad pitches to bowl on, he bowled quite a lot, and took sixty-three wickets, average under twenty. I saw him take a wicket in his last full season, when he had Langdale of Somerset, who had scored 146, leg-before. His delight was plain to see, and shared by all present (Somerset supporters could afford to smile, as they had made nearly 500). He smiled more often when taking a wicket than when making a century, especially as he grew older and heavier.

Robertson-Glasgow wrote one of his best essays about Leyland, concluding with a quotation from Dr Johnson: 'Any violence offered me I shall do my best to repel. I shall not be deterred by the menaces of a ruffian. Your rage I defy. Your abilities are not so formidable. I pay regard not to what you say, but to what you shall prove.'

Cardus also wrote beautifully about Leyland on several occasions. In his report of the 1938 Oval Test, he imagined Leyland in verbal communion with the bowlers. He played O'Reilly 'with a rich, comic, wooden sort of assurance, as though saying all the time, "Hey, Bill, tha'rt a good un, but Ah know all about thi." So Fleetwood-Smith came to O'Reilly's assistance, and Leyland hit his first ball for four, as though continuing his discourse "And tha'rt not what I'd call surprising, either." '

When Leyland had scored seventy runs, he played a false stroke as though saying, 'Go on, lads, get me out – it can be done; Ah'm playing for mi place in t'team, remember.' And when Leyland was bowled by a no-ball from O'Reilly, Cardus imagined him saying 'Live and let live; give him a bit of encouragement – it costs nowt.'

He was sometimes called by his Yorkshire colleagues 'Tonnip'. This I presume was a Yorkshire pronunciation of 'turnip', not that there was anything vegetable-like about him, but it did suggest the gentle, slow-spoken country boy, not tall, bottle-shaped shoulders, big bottom. This was the appearance he gave, though he was born in Harrogate, not quite the depths of the country. Possibly there may have been another derivation. J. H. Vaux, in 'A New and Comprehensive Dictionary of the Flash Language', 1812, says that 'to give anybody turnips signifies to turn him or her up, and the party so turned up is said to have knap'd turnips'. Vaux is pretty good at north country slang, and Leyland was pretty good at turning a match upside down. O'Reilly must often have felt that he had been knap'd.

Leyland was Yorkshire's coach from 1951 to 1963, and it was in those years that I met him several times, and occasionally chatted to him. He then had to retire, through illness, a long and painful illness – though he would struggle along if Yorkshire were playing at Harrogate or not too far away. He died much too soon in 1967. I think the last time I saw him was at Harrogate in 1965, when Yorkshire beat Gloucestershire by an innings and fifty-two. He seemed a little gloomy. He did not think it was a good Yorkshire side, nothing to compare with the side of the 1930s (just as in the 1930s Yorkshiremen said that the side led by Sellers was nothing to compare with the side led by Hawke at the beginning of the century). I have looked up the names of that Yorkshire side at Harrogate: Boycott, Hampshire, Padgett, Close, Sharpe, Illingworth, Richard Hutton, Binks, Trueman, Don Wilson and Nicholson. The first ten all played for England, and so would Nicholson have done but for an injury. Yet Leyland, despite the entirely proper depression at the lack of talent in his native county, always kept up his spirits and the spirits of those about him.

As the careers of Sutcliffe and Leyland drew towards their close, we began to hear predictions of a young Yorkshire batsman who would turn out to be better than either. In his book, Sutcliffe had written of Hutton, then only 18, that 'He is a marvel – the discovery of a generation.' Lord Hawke, who wrote the preface, thought that Sutcliffe was overdoing it: 'I hope he has not formed too high an opinion of Hutton's ability.' Sir Home Gordon, who provided the statistics for the book, also expressed the view that Sutcliffe's confident prophecies were too burdensome for the lad. Sutcliffe would not be budged. Hutton came from Pudsey, as Sutcliffe had done (and before them Tunnicliffe and Booth, and afterwards Illingworth). When he began to join Sutcliffe in opening the Yorkshire innings, there was a feeling of *post hoc ergo propter hoc*, though I do not suppose they put it quite that way in Pudsey. When Sutcliffe wrote that 'This boy will be a power in the land before many moons, and I shall not be surprised to find him attracting as much attention as any batsman, including the great Don, for his style and polished skill must triumph', we thought, even we enthusiastic Yorkshire boys, that Sutcliffe was affectionately piling it on a bit. But in 1938, after Hutton had beaten Bradman's Test record against Australia, P. F. Warner, who had been on the sceptical side, wrote that 'He has justified every word his mentor said about him.'

Yet Sutcliffe was not exactly Hutton's 'mentor', not the guide and advisor to the young Telemachus. He did not coach Hutton, though his example from the other end of the pitch must have counted for much. In later years, Hutton did not seem all that pleased that he was assumed so readily to be Sutcliffe's child. I once heard him say that the only cricketer who ever taught him anything was George Hirst at the Headingley nets. Hirst was a great coach, but was born in 1871, and by the time Hutton started can only have been a peripheral influence. This may have been one of Hutton's cryptic little jokes, but he has always been his own man: a man slightly apart. He had his own genius for the game, and if you think 'genius' is too strong a word, let us settle for Sutcliffe's 'marvel'.

In 1936 Hutton became a regular member of the Yorkshire side, scored nearly 1300 runs, and was awarded his county cap. There was a thought that he might be taken to Australia that autumn. R. E. S. Wyatt, a very good judge of a player (though sometimes eccentric in his captaincy decisions on the field) considered he should have been, certainly once the decision had been taken to drop Sutcliffe. Wyatt also thought it might have been a good idea to take Compton, who was even younger than Hutton – but neither suggestion seems to have been very seriously considered at the time.

It was in the autumn of 1936 that I first went away to school, and I was so miserably unhappy there for six months or so that I really took very little interest at the time in the Australian tour that winter. However, at Taunton, I found myself with many more Yorkshire allies among my contemporaries than I had ever had in London. There was a strong Somerset element of course. The day boys were almost unanimously for Somerset. But the boarders came from all over the place. The Yorkshire contingent was substantial and we drew together tykishly in summer, rejoicing or mourning as circumstances required. It was mostly rejoicing at that time, and we were certainly not bothered by Somerset, then inconsiderable in championship terms. The cricket season of 1937, and the stout Yorkshire companionship with which I entered it, did much to reconcile me to my surroundings, though I still disliked them. But

I began to see that school need not be altogether horrible. Getting in the house second eleven helped too.

It was an important year for Yorkshire in 1937. They won the championship in the end, narrowly, after a struggle with Middlesex which, Jim Swanton wrote, 'stirred the emotions of North and South as they had not been stirred since Warner's last summer' (that was in 1920, when Lancashire and Middlesex had been the rivals). It was an important year for Hutton. We followed the progress of the predicted prodigy with acute anxiety. He did well in the early games, and was chosen for the first Test against New Zealand.

I knew there had been a disaster when at lunchtime I saw the face of a fellow Yorkshireman on the other side of a quadrangle. He had been listening to a wireless. As we approached one another, he had no words to speak: he lifted up his right hand, and formed his thumb and first finger into a nought. I remember this chap's name, Walton. He was, at that stage of his career, known as 'Piggy' Walton. This was not, I think, any reflection on his appearance, but possibly on his appetite. I shall always be grateful to him for his consideration at that moment of anguish. We went to the tuckshop, not that we had funds for a spread, but something had to be done to fill in the empty moments. We communed, as silently as boys of that age ever do, over a Mars bar and a still lemonade each. We endeavoured to cheer ourselves up with the thought of the second innings.

In the second innings Hutton scored one.

It was their fast bowler called Cowie who got him out both times. It was a great pity that we did not see more of Cowie in England. He did not come again until 1949 when he was past his best. But he got Hutton out for a third time in the 1937 series, and a fourth time in 1949. In his first four Tests against the great man he had him out four times, though Hutton had evened the balance by the end.

However, Piggy and I were in no mood to harp on the merits of Cowie at that time. We were secretly afraid that our hero might be dropped for the next Test, though publicly we scoffed at the suggestion. We did not want the selectors to get the idea that there was any doubt, any defeatism in the hearts of the small Yorkshire boys of Taunton School. In this endeavour we were successful, for he was chosen again and scored a hundred. By the end of the season he had scored 2888 runs, average nearly 57. His only rival among the younger generation of batsmen was Compton, who also had a successful season, and was chosen for the last Test. So we had a couple of rods in pickle for the 1938 Australians (I dare say we even used that phrase: birch rods used to be laid in brine to keep the twigs pliable, and though we did not have a birch at Taunton, there was still a good deal of corporal punishment, and I remember that a beating was sometimes called a 'pickling').

But before I continue with an account of Hutton's progress, I must say a little more about the climax to that 1937 season. It had been a close thing most of the time. Yorkshire lagged at the beginning, partly because of an injury to Bowes, their fast bowler. But they caught up, and in the last few weeks the lead kept changing hands. Yorkshire were captained by Sellers, Middlesex by Robins. Yorkshire looked the stronger side on the face of it – nearly all of them past or future Test players. Middlesex could match them in captaincy, in batting (as well as Compton, there was Edrich, and, in his last season, still highly effective, Hendren) but hardly in bowling, once Bowes was fit. Yet Robins kept pulling out tricks, and in the middle of August they were ahead. To re-capture the lead Yorkshire had to beat Glamorgan, and from the wireless news on the third afternoon they did not look like doing it.

We were on holiday that year at Swanage. I can't think why. We usually went to St Ives or Grange-over-Sands. Perhaps my boarding fees were making a dent in the family income. Swanage was all right – I have always liked the place, and the Isle of Purbeck – but it was not a very successful holiday, chiefly because we had unsatisfactory digs. The grub was poor and we were too far from the beach. That evening, after the depressing wireless news, father set out for the long walk to the bowling green on the front. Mother and I followed an hour or so later. When we glimpsed father, some distance away, he had finished his game and was poring over an evening newspaper. When he saw us he began waving the newspaper over his head. Mother said, 'Look! Look at Dad! They must have won!' I raced ahead of her, and discovered that yes, they had won. I have always felt warmly towards Glamorgan cricket, but never more so than for that timely collapse. A bowler, seeing father's newspaper, came to the edge of the green, jack in hand, and asked politely, tensely, if he knew the Yorkshire result. When told, he cried, 'Confound it!' with quite surprising venom for a stately man with stately manners, and flung the jack on the ground.

I have toyed since with the thought that he might have been Jim Swanton, but the evidence is against it. I recall the incident to illustrate how high feelings were running.

So Yorkshire were on top of the table with only a few matches to go. But next morning we discovered, from the newspapers, that if both sides won all their remaining matches, Middlesex would be champions. It did not seem impossible that this would happen. They were better than any other of the counties they would play, and the weather was set fair. The championship was then decided on percentages, and Middlesex played only twenty-four matches to Yorkshire's twenty-eight: so every Middlesex win would raise their percentage more highly than a Yorkshire win.

'Dirty work', I thought, as I walked gloomily around Peveril Point that morning. I longed for the presence of Piggy Walton, whom I knew would be sharing my wrath. Father had shaken his head on reading the news, and even pursed his lips, but perhaps he felt he had done enough by waving his newspaper at the quasi-Jim Swanton the previous evening, and he was never a man to join in a demo. To me, however, it was clear that this state of affairs was fixed by the people at Lord's, who hated northerners, in order to win Middlesex the championship. I was not the only Yorkshire supporter to feel this way. Yorkshire had played Middlesex twice that season. Middlesex had won once, and taken first innings points in the other. They had had the better of the weather and the luck. The thought that, now they had been overhauled, they might still get away with it, simply by playing fewer matches, was unbearable to any Yorkshireman; and as I have had occasion to observe before, nearly all Yorkshiremen are Latin Americans under the skin.

Robins sensed the northern resentment, which was soon reciprocated in the south, and being a brave, generous and imaginative man, sent a telegram to Sellers, challenging Yorkshire to a four-day match on neutral ground for the end of the season, irrespective of the championship result. Sellers immediately accepted, adding belligerently to his telegram '£10 a man'. The last clause, which I believe had originally been suggested by Maurice Leyland, was subsequently withdrawn at the behest of the Yorkshire committee, who declared piously that they disapproved of betting on cricket. But the challenge was on, and a good deal more than £10 a man must have changed hands on the result. Had it not been for the strict prohibition on betting in my family (it was a worse crime than reading a Sunday paper) I would have had a bob or so on Yorkshire myself.

In the last week of the championship, Middlesex had to play Nottinghamshire at Trent Bridge and Surrey at Lord's: Yorkshire were on what used to be called in those more spacious days their 'southern tour', playing Sussex at Eastbourne and Hampshire at Bournemouth. Yorkshire beat Sussex easily, Verity being surprisingly destructive on the Saffrons pitch, rarely a help to spinners. But it looked as if Middlesex would win too. After Nottinghamshire had scored 316, they declared at 525 on the second evening, and captured some early wickets in the Nottinghamshire second innings. Reading the evening paper, I found a touch of hope in that Hardstaff was not out at lunch. He went on to make 200, and the match was drawn. This meant that Yorkshire had only to beat Hampshire to be champions, and they did without much difficulty. Middlesex could only draw in a high scoring match at Lord's, so there was a respectable gap between first and second at the end.

There followed the challenge match at the Oval. It was subsequently referred to as an anticlimax, and looking back down the years I can see that it was, except for your partisan Yorkshireman, partly because Middlesex were without several regular players, including Compton. Yorkshire won the toss, scored 400 and won by an innings, with some help from rain. But it did create interest at the time, there were large crowds on the first two days, and Cardus wrote some admirable reports of it. So far as I know, these have not been reprinted, and I commend them to Margaret Hughes, who has presided zealously and affectionately over the preservation of the best of his journalism in a series of books. For me, the challenge match was an unalloyed joy, the crowning mercy of a memorable season.

But *revenons à notre Hutton*. In 1938 he scored a century in the first Test against Australia (as Compton did). In the second he made only four and five, in trouble against McCormick, an Australian bowler who was erratic but very fast for a few overs. The third Test was a washout. The fourth Hutton could not play in because of an injury. He returned for the fifth, and made the famous 364.

Now I saw most of the first two days of this match, or at least was present. I was then rather small for my age and had an impeded view. Nor was I used to big crowds. My recollections of the occasion were more confused, and less pleasant, than those of the

555 by Holmes and Sutcliffe. Big chaps with Elephant and Castle voices and pints in their hands kept shoving me out of the way. Nevertheless, there was always the scoreboard, visible with its assurance that Hutton was still in. On the third day, with Hutton 300 not out, the family left for a holiday in the north (back to good old Grange-over-Sands), and it was, I think at Rugby (or it may conceivably have been Stafford) that, leaning out of the carriage window, I learnt from a porter that Bradman's record had been surpassed.

This 364 is not nowadays reckoned one of the greatest Test innings, not even one of Hutton's best, though it is still the highest between England and Australia. Jack Fingleton once said that 'Hutton was far too good a batsman to have played it', but he said it with a twinkle, and he had been in the field for most of the thirteen hours odd it took. But quite soon, as Edmund Blunden noted in *Cricket Country*, there was a reaction against it, and against England's massive victory, among the sophisticated. Blunden wrote:

> Scarcely greater shaking of heads and murmurings of dissatis-
> faction had been noticeable when our own team was being put
> through the mill in Australia. Something must be wrong! and
> even Hutton's innings was not quite so full-heartedly enjoyed in
> afterthought as it was at the time, while the collective achieve-
> ment of W. R. Hammond's team was referred to rather as though
> it had been an illegal or discreditable business.

But for me, and most other boys (not just Yorkshire boys), and come to that for most English cricketers of any age, if they were honest about their feelings, bliss was it in that dawn to be alive. We had suffered so much from all those years of Bradman.

I wish I had been there at the transcendent moment, but I was content with Cardus's description.

> Thousands of happy people stood up and cheered. Somebody
> with a cornet began to play 'For he's a jolly good fellow!' and the
> crowd took up the refrain in that evangelical tone which the
> British public invariably adopts when it lifts up its heart to
> rejoice in song. Moreover, the voices and the cornet did not
> keep together – but in the circumstances I admit that to say so is
> a piece of pedantic musical criticism. Bradman shook hands
> with the hero, all the Australians shook hands with him,

journeying to the wicket from the remoter parts of the Oval – all except tired Bill O'Reilly, who lay prone on the grass until he saw a man coming out with drinks, when he got up at once and made for him in a hurry . . . Hutton took the occasion with a charming modesty. He raised his cap in the acknowledgment of the honours done to him, and bent his head. But what a moment for him! – the moment of his life.

Well, so it was, and yet the innings brought its problems for Hutton. Inevitably, and not only by the small boys, he was expected to go on scoring in such vast quantities, and he never had the physique for it. Even Sutcliffe, in all his enthusiasm for the young master, had slipped in the qualification, 'Given good health . . .' and Hutton was never a robust man. But all was well for the time, and he had a marvellous season in 1939, which I have heard him say was his best. We had thought of him as a cautious batsman and were to do so again, but that year he played all his strokes, and his runs came mostly at a great pace. Sellers at one time felt constrained to issue a mild warning, suggesting that seventy or eighty before lunch was all very well, but a shade rash for a Yorkshire opener. And Len politely agreed, and, in the words of Sellers, 'went on doing it just the same'. Only the outbreak of war prevented him from reaching 3000 runs. This feat he was only to achieve once in 1949 when he made 3429. In that year he scored a thousand runs in June, and a thousand in August. His June figure, 1194, included three consecutive ducks, which really is a record worth remembering, and unlikely to be equalled.

During the war, while serving in the Army, Hutton had an unlucky accident in a gymnasium. His left wrist was broken, and several operations failed to put it sufficiently together again. It was thought that he might not play any more first-class cricket, and I can remember how shocked I was after the war at Oxford to see his left arm, when he had taken off the protector. 'It's bloody withered', whispered an equally shocked New Zealander beside me. This was too strong a word, but the ultimate result of the operations was that his left arm was shortened by an inch. You would have thought it impossible for a man whose play was founded on the classical off-drive to be so good again after so crucial a misfortune. It was. He was never *quite* so good again, but good enough to be, for several years after Bradman retired, the best batsman in the world.

I must add that you would also have thought it impossible for a man so dependent upon his dancing leg-work as Compton to be so good again after his knee had gone a few years later. Again it was, but only just. Despite all his triumphs, after his mighty season in 1947 (he still holds the records for the number of runs, and the number of centuries in a season) Compton was never *quite* so good again. That he was never, before or after the accidents, quite so good as Hutton, was for me a matter of faith rather than judgment. Often I have wondered what would have happened had it been Compton's arm and Hutton's knee to suffer, instead of the other way round. I suspect that they would have been even more formidable.

However, Hutton had an acceptable season in 1946, and naturally went with Hammond's team to Australia the following winter. There he had what would have been considered an excellent tour had he been anyone else. He averaged seventy in all first-class matches, and led the Test match averages with fifty-two. He had to retire in the last Test when he was 122 not out, and return home early for an operation for tonsillitis. Yet he began the 1947 season in such form that people were talking about a thousand runs in May. But his health was telling upon him, and although he scored 2500 runs by the end, he did no better than all right in the Tests against South Africa, and it was the summer of Compton and Edrich. You must remember that an eager public in the north was still expecting him to score a hundred a time; and an equally eager public in the south was glad of any evidence that Compton was the better bat. I was a grown-up by this time and should have shed these childish pains. I was conscious of my responsibility as cricket correspondent for *Isis*, but if I managed to repress my bias in print, it would burst out later in the evening after a few pints in the buttery at Queen's. I was un-regenerate.

In 1948, having given us a good licking over there, the Australians arrived to repeat the process. Compton played what must have been two of the best innings of his life, 184 in the first Test, and 145 not out, after being cut over in the third. Hutton played a valuable second innings in the first Test, seventy-four, after being out for three in the first. On both occasions he was bowled by Miller. In the second Test he scored twenty and thirteen. Lindwall and Miller had the advantage of a new ball every fifty-five overs. He did not rise to the occasion at Lord's. Of his second innings J. M. Kilburn, a devoted admirer, wrote that 'Leonard gave the most disappointing personal display of his career'. He was dropped for the third Test. This was the only time he was left out of an England side when fit and available.

My indignation knew no bounds. My cheeks still flush, partly from shame, but partly from recalled wrath, as I cast my mind back. Dirty work by Lord's again! But the reasoning of the England selectors was that they had a weak batting side, were up against two very fast bowlers (with Bill Johnstone, who could also be quick when he chose, in support) and that if their number one backed away, as he had done in the second Test – I was not there, but it has to be accepted – the effect on the rest would be disastrous. Jim Swanton told me many years later that though he was as surprised as anyone else at the decision, he felt it had proved wise, if only because 'I never saw Len flinch again for the rest of his career.'

Back for the fourth Test after Emmett's unhappy interlude, Hutton scored 81 and 57, and in the fifth 30 (out of a total of 52) and 64 (out of 188, again the highest score). Kilburn wrote of this match that 'Len alone looked as though his strokes were of his own choice, and made in his own time', a reassurance possibly intended for himself as much as his readers. All the same, Compton headed the averages.

Hutton had not really compared with him, and Yorkshiremen ruefully felt at the end of that season that they did not, after all, possess the best English batsman. This changed in the next few years, partly because of Compton's knee. Hutton had a successful tour of South Africa in the winter, scored his 3429 in 1949, including 206 against New Zealand at the Oval: and in 1950 again at the Oval carried his bat through the innings for 206 against the West Indies. In 1950–51 he had his best Test season. His average in Australia was sixty-six for all matches, and in Tests eighty-nine. Only Hammond had ever averaged higher for England over there, in 1928–9 when runs were more plentiful. Hutton's average was helped by four not outs, but that was partly because his captain, F. R. Brown, had put him down the order for the first two Tests (this was not a slur on Hutton, but an attempt, unsuccessful but not altogether irrational, to strengthen the middle batting). In the fourth Test at Adelaide Hutton carried his bat through a Test innings for the second time in six months, for 156. The next batsman in the Test averages was Simpson, thirty-nine. Washbrook averaged seventeen, Compton eight.

That was the peak of Hutton's career so far as batting went. But the succession to the captaincy now had to be considered. Brown carried on against South Africa in 1951 and then retired. India were here in 1952. The selectors – Yardley, Wyatt, Brown and Ames – took the plunge and chose a professional. A quarter of a century later it seems an obvious enough decision, but goodness it caused a stir then, not only the principle but the particular choice. Compton had been vice-captain to Brown on the 1950–51 tour, and presumably was intended as his successor when the dread moment came; but Compton had not shone as a captain, and Australians as well as Englishmen noted that Brown seemed to rely chiefly for advice on Hutton. I have always thought that Brown had more to do with Hutton's appointment than anyone.

I have written at some length, in *The Cricket Captains of England*, about Hutton's Test captaincy, so here I merely summarise the story. He won easily enough against India in 1952, and then won the last, deciding Test at the Oval against Australia in 1953. His batting did not decline with the responsibility as noticeably as had been predicted. His 145 at Lord's was one of his best – Jack Fingleton said that it was the best he ever saw him play – and at the Oval his eighty-two was the highest innings of the match. He might have been out early, when his cap (the same one that he had worn there in 1938) was knocked off by a flier from Lindwall, and nearly fell on the stumps.

That winter there was to be a tour of the West Indies. There were still those who thought that while a professional captain in England might be feasible, a professional captain on tour was something else again, but Hutton's position was beyond challenge. Yet the critical voices were heard again when he came home after a drawn rubber. England had been two down, but won two out of the last three. The recovery was principally due to the batting of the captain, who averaged 150 in the last three, though it was Bailey's best (ever) spell of bowling (16–7–34–7) in the last match which gave England the chance of saving the rubber. It was not a specially happy tour, though happier than many which have taken place since. At Georgetown bottles were thrown on the field, and it was described as a riot, though it has been surpassed frequently (even Sunday afternoons at such traditionally peaceful grounds as Taunton and Worcester have managed passable imitations). Elegant ladies complained that English cricketers had molested them, and E. W. Swanton had to be called in as arbiter – I suspect he rather enjoyed it, for the corridors of power have always fitted comfortably his stately form. There was a misunderstanding between Hutton and the chief minister of Jamaica, Mr Bustamante. Hutton's senior professionals did not co-operate so much as they might have done, at least in the earlier part of the tour. He had not been given the right manager. So at the end of it all, it was not uncommon to hear such phrases as 'Told you so. Professional captains abroad simply won't do.'

Then in 1954 when Pakistan were our visitors, Hutton was unwell for much of the time, and able to play only in the first Test and the last (which we lost). In his absence David Sheppard was made captain, and there was some idea that he might be the best choice to captain England in Australia in the 1954–55 side. This was – it was blandly said – in order to allow Hutton to concentrate on his batting, as though the poor man had not scored a run in the West Indies.

I was angry at such suggestions. I knew David Sheppard a little, because we had broadcast together several times in such programmes as *Christian Forum*, and liked and admired him very much, both as a man and a cricketer. His evangelical and ecumenical approach to the Christian faith has always been close to my own. He would have made a splendid captain of England in Australia, and should probably have been appointed to the job eight years later, when he took a sabbatical and made the tour, though Dexter was preferred as captain. But no, not in 1954. Hutton had to be the captain on that tour, and he had to retain the Ashes for the credit of professional and Yorkshire cricket. I am trying to recall my feelings at the time, you understand. One evening, before the selection had been announced, I took the chair in a programme called 'Sporting Fanfare', a kind of sports attempt to imitate 'Any Questions?' and the matter of the captaincy was inevitably raised. John Arlott spoke up for Hutton. Rex Alston spoke up for Sheppard. I could hardly bring myself to speak to Rex over the subsequent glass or two, and very possibly I may have given myself away during the programme. I was not at all a suitable man to be taking the chair in such a programme at that time.

I should have been ashamed of myself at my age, and indeed these were the last agonies of parturition. Hutton took the side to Australia, and won the rubber, after putting in the Australians in the first Test, and losing by an innings. By the end of the series, it was a comfortable win. Hutton did not bat so well, though he scored eighty in the fourth Test, the one which settled the rubber: the highest score of the match. His last Test was played on the way home against New Zealand and won by an innings, and again he was the highest England scorer. It was hoped that he might lead us against the Australians in 1956, but after a few matches in 1955 he retired: gracefully, without rancour, but looking a little worn. In trying to assess his career as an England captain, I wrote that:

> The conflict with Lindwall and Miller provides the key . . . What was needed to win Test matches, he decided, was two fast bowlers, a judgement which history, before and since, has generally confirmed. He thought at first that his fast bowlers were to be Trueman and Statham. After Trueman's disappointing season in the West Indies, they turned out, in Australia, to be Tyson and Statham. Hutton's difficulty was that Bedser, who had taken 30 wickets against Australia in 1950–1, and 39 in 1953, had a prescriptive right to the new ball.

After the disastrous first Test, he retired from public view for a few days, and emerged with what Jack Fingleton called 'the terrific decision' to omit Bedser. He did not, however, inform Bedser of the decision until he posted the team on the dressing room board. This was rightly held to be an error in captaincy, though the selection was justified when it came to the match. Communication with his colleagues was never his strongest point. Nevertheless, he was the only captain this century to win two consecutive rubbers against Australia, at full strength. Chapman won at home in 1926, and away in 1928–9, but was only captain in the last match in 1926. Warner did, in 1903–4, and 1911–12, but was taken ill on the second tour and could not play in a Test. More recently, Brearley did, but his away tour, because of all the Packer business, was not won against the strongest possible Australian side. Do not think this a disparagement of Brearley. I am inclined to think that he was the best captain, *qua* captain, that England has ever had. His difficulty was that he was – no, not an amateur in the sense of being unpaid, but in the amateur tradition, Cambridge and all that. Hutton's difficulty was that he was a professional, the first in the job. *Autres temps, autres moeurs*. They were different difficulties, different by a generation. Hutton was a firm choice for England on merit as a cricketer, Brearley often a doubtful one. So if I was making out a list of the best all-round English captains, I would still place Sir Leonard at the top.

But even as I write these words, I can feel a tinge of the old love and hate recurring. No more than a tinge. When Hutton retired, sufficed by success, my last hero, I also retired from partisanship. I felt, as in a different sense he did, that nothing could better that 1954–55 season in Australia, and that all ambition achieved, all passion spent, I could sit back and enjoy the game for a change.

When I was a small boy in Ilkley we had a china cabinet in a corner of the drawing room (the drawing room, you understand, was the posh room, only used on Sunday afternoons, or when distinguished visitors came). The cabinet contained, apart from some inherited bits of silver, I expect EPNS, a complete tea set of elegant china. There were pink and yellow roses round the rim. I still possess a couple of pieces from the set, the last remnants. This had been a wedding present, and mother was so proud of it that she would never take it out of the cabinet, in case it got broken. One afternoon she did, because the president of the Baptist Union came to tea. It thereafter became known as 'The president of the Baptist Union's china', and I am glad to say that another president of the Baptist Union ate a sandwich from one of the surviving plates, half a century later. But I digress. What I meant to say, and indeed have said before, was that I never much enjoyed watching Hutton bat. I was always scared he might get out, just as mother was always scared what might happen to the best china if she took it out of the cabinet.

XII

Slaves of the Lamp

Nor ever once ashamed
So we be named
Press-men; Slaves of the Lamp; Servants of Light.
Edwin Arnold

It was odd, the way my cricketing life worked out. It was also, I am inclined to think, fortunate. For as my partisan passions withered, I became increasingly involved in the game professionally. For fourteen years I did occasional radio commentary, here and there. Other regions were sometimes kind enough to invite me, and I remember in particular one trip to Blackpool, where I met many of father's family, including a cousin of exceptional beauty, whom I had last seen when she was about six – nobody, as I proudly took her out to dinner, believed for a moment that she was my cousin. I also remember happy days in Scotland and Ireland. Noble Wilson, then a senior outside broadcasts producer in Glasgow, took me, with his wife, to a picnic on the banks of Loch Lomond one summer evening. The sun was falling as he drove us home, and I began the Tennyson bit:

> *The splendour falls on castle walls*

– and at once they joined in –

> *And snowy summits old in story*
> *The long light shakes across the lakes*
> *And the wild cataract foams in glory.*

I am not sure how much of it we managed to remember, but we certainly got in 'The horns of Elfland'. It was one of those moments, the place and the words and the friends, which stir the soul. I have met Noble and his wife, who for some obscure reason is called Leafy, often since, but mostly when he was the BBC representative in Paris, very posh. I am sure he did this and subsequent jobs very well, but I shall remember him for that picnic on the bonny banks.

And I remember an Irish moment. I had happy days with Irish cricket especially at Castle Avenue, Dublin. On one occasion a touring side were playing Ireland in two consecutive one-day matches, the first at Dublin and the second at Belfast. Charles Freer, the outside broadcasts producer for Northern Ireland, drove me north on the first evening. It was the first time I had taken that road, and I saw some dark hills ahead, sharp against the evening sky. And what are they, I enquired innocently and ignorantly? 'Think of your Irish history, your Irish poetry', said Charles, sternly for him. They were the Mountains of Mourne. This was just before the Troubles began again. I had dinner that evening with Charles and his son, and I asked them whether they saw any signs of unrest in the north. 'No', said Charles, confidently. 'Belfast is a relaxed city.' His son, under 20, added sharply, 'But there *is* discrimination.' They were a Church of Ireland family. Whenever they passed through Newry, I think it was, the cry would go up, 'That's one of ours!' as a Church of Ireland building hove into view. But this was just a family joke. Irish cricket, like Irish rugby, has remained undivided. I once asked at Castle Avenue why this should be so, when there are two Irish soccer teams, who could conceivably meet one day in the final of the World Cup, a thought that beggars imagination. The general feeling was summed up in a phrase by Charles, 'Probably because such bloody silly people run Irish soccer.'

A good deal of nonsense has been written about the supposed influence for international amity exerted by international sport. Orwell wrote in 1945:

If you wanted to add to the vast fund of ill-will existing in the world at this moment, you could hardly do it better than by a series of football matches between Jews and Arabs, Germans and Czechs, Indians and British, Russians and Poles, and Italians and Jugoslavs, each match to be watched by a mixed audience of 100,000 spectators. I do not, of course, suggest that sport is one of the main causes of international rivalry; big-scale sport is itself, I think, merely another effect of the causes that have produced nationalism. Still, you do make things worse by sending forth a team of eleven men, labelled as national champions, to do battle against some rival team, and allowing it to be felt on all sides that whichever nation is defeated will 'lose face'.

Every year that has passed has confirmed the wisdom of those words. Orwell was writing about football because he was concerned with the recent tour of Britain by Moscow Dynamo, but he knew about cricket as well – indeed he was fond of cricket, and though never very good at it used to watch it a lot. Cricket has, more than any game, been held up as a contribution to the brotherhood of man. Yet I should say that relations between England and Australia have been as much damaged as strengthened by Test matches, at least in the last half century. But we must always remember the healing example of Ireland – in this respect at least, it has shone like a good deed in a naughty world. I was delighted when Ireland were admitted to the Gillette Cup in 1980, and gave the mighty Middlesex a fright at Lord's.

In such ways my cricketing experience gradually widened. In 1962 I had joined the radio Test match panel, and stayed with it, off and on, for fifteen years. This meant watching cricket more seriously and extensively. Then, in the early 1970s, the West of England Home Service lamentably came to an end, and the larger part of my living went with it. I have written about the personal problems of those years elsewhere. All I need to say in this context is that by chance rather than choice, I became a journalist rather than a broadcaster, and principally a cricket journalist. I still was able to live in the west, and saw plenty of the western counties, but I had to travel much more. In the summer I did very little else but report cricket, and so it has continued. I do not complain about this as a way of buying the bread, though it is not quite the idle bask in the sunshine which those who have never tried it envisage. Cricket is time consuming. Travel is wearying as you grow older, home is tempting, words come less readily, the telephone service does not improve. The hardest part of the day's work, usually, is telephoning the copy through.

This must not be taken as a criticism of the copytakers. *The Times* has always set a high standard in this respect. When I began writing regularly for them the principal copytaker was Laurie Wayman, who was so good at his job, and made himself so indispensable in other respects, that at one time he seemed to be running the entire sports department. You never had to spell out a name with Laurie. He knew them all. If you committed a grammatical error, or a solecism such as repeating an adjective, he would gently draw it to your attention ('Have I got that quite right, Mr Gibson?'). Long ago, I was sent to report the Fijians playing at Maesteg. It was the first rugby tour by the Fijians, and their first match. They played excitingly well, and I began my report with a quotation:

> 'Then felt I like some watcher of the skies
> When a new planet swims into his ken;
> Or like stout Cortez, when with eagle eyes
> He gazed at the Pacific'

– it was not quite so mannered as it reads now, because it really had been a surprise, and the Pacific was to the point. But, feeling pleased with myself, I was brought down from such flights by Laurie's gentle voice: 'Shouldn't that word be "stared", Mr Gibson?' He hastened on apologetically, 'Not sure myself. Forgotten most of my Keats.' I think I realised then, more than I had ever done before, the aweful responsibility of writing for *The Times*. Although Laurie now works for *The Times* only occasionally, much of his style persists – indeed, much of his accent, for several of the others sound very like him. I have never written for a newspaper where the standard of copytaking approached *The Times*. Certainly not *The Sunday Times*, though the pressures there are higher on those desperate Saturday evenings. The *Sunday* has taken to employing women copytakers, which is not often a good idea for cricket and rugby. I suppose the vague idea behind it is that women are less liable to go on strike suddenly than men, and heaven knows how the *Sunday* has suffered from industrial disputes, but not many women play cricket, and hardly any at all rugby, and they cannot be expected to be familiar with the technical terms. *The Sunday Times* has been very loyal to me, and indeed I hope I to them, but it is a difficult paper for which to write. They like their reports early. Their ideal cricket report would be one which was sent through just after the captains had tossed for innings, and before your actual play had started – always on condition that it was, in a favourite phrase of theirs, 'a full rounded report'. As, for instance, 'It was a notable day at Lord's, as we knew it would be when Brearley won the toss, and after what must have been considerable meditation, decided to bat. This decision, we may say with all the confidence of a passenger who resolves never again to change at Didcot, governed the ensuing events. There was a touch of green in the wicket, and a touch of blue in the sky. It was good to see a touch of red in the face of Bill Alley, as that familiar ruddy face once more led Tetbury plumber Sam Cook, his fellow-umpire, and the Northamptonshire eleven on to the field. Northamptonshire were without Dye, which will prove to be a handicap to them at some stage of the match. Alley was, as usual, one of the dominant figures of the day, beneath a sun which was both changing and unchanging. Brearley, as he made ready to open the batting, wore his usual quirky, confident grin. And was he, at the end of the long day, pleased with his initial decision? Only he can say, and he is not likely to reveal his inmost thoughts – he has never been a man for that. We can, however, have no doubt that some aspects of the play must have gratified him, even if others did not.'

There you are, and I have just typed it out in about five minutes, 200 words or so of the best bejewelled prose, and *rounded*, and not a ball bowled. All you need to fill in is the scorecard, which they take from the Press Association anyway. Whatever score they set down will fit that report. Of course sometimes odd things happen, so you might need an extra sentence at lunchtime for the late London edition: such as 'Brearley must have been gratified, for instance, by his hundred before lunch', or 'One of Brearley's disappointments must have been that first ball he took a thumper in the crutch, and inadvertently sat on his wicket'. But barring such emergencies, you were all right with that first paragraph for *The Sunday Times*. The sports page is less ambitious now, but they did try very hard for a long time to give detailed regional coverage. What let them down was not their editing, but their distribution. I gave up the paper when my edition in Somerset carried the banner headline, 'RANGERS WIN, CELTIC DRAW'. Doubtless in Glasgow they were puzzling over my thoughts on Plymouth Albion v. Cheltenham.

All that said, I do not deny that on the whole, the lot has fallen unto me in a fair ground: yea, I have a goodly heritage. I do find, however, that the more cricket I see, the less I remember. I could give you a far more detailed account of, say, England v. South Africa at Lord's in 1951, though I was only there in patches as a spectator, than of many Tests I have seen at Lord's in the last twenty years, even though I have conscientiously watched nearly every ball of them. Willie Watson of Yorkshire played a handsome innings in that match, and Ray Tattersall of Lancashire took a lot of wickets. Neither of these men had very much luck with the England selectors. I felt this keenly in the case of Watson, who seemed to score runs whenever I was present – it is one of the hazards of judging a cricketer that some always seem to come off before your very eyes, some never. I took much convincing of the merits of Keith Fletcher, for instance, because for several years my arrival at a ground where he was playing was the signal for him to get out, or drop a catch in the slips.

Memory fails as you grow older. This is not just a matter of age, but of the quantity of information it has to consume. When I saw perhaps half a dozen first-class matches a season, I could still recall much of the detail over many years. Now, the match is over, the report written and (much more difficult) telephoned. I am on the train back to Bath, day's work done. You dismiss it from your mind, and if some fellow traveller asks the score, have to look up your notes to be sure. If you think about cricket at all, it is to wonder where you are going tomorrow. Worcester? Damn. It means the 7.53 from Bristol, changing at Gloucester (an hour's wait) and still arriving at Worcester nearly an hour before the start of play. You can while away the time at Worcester by visiting the cathedral, and you can at Gloucester too (though it is a long way from the station, and there are never any taxis at the new Gloucester station). Besides, you cannot always be in a prayerful or architectural mood. The next train from Bristol leaves Bristol at 11.25, and does not get you to the ground until the middle of the lunch interval: that is, provided it isn't late, and you have remembered to ring up Golden Wings (one of the most reliable taxi firms I have encountered) to meet it and wait for it. Well, there will be good friends in the Worcester press box, who will 'fill you in', as the phrase goes. Besides, it might rain. Clouds there in the west you notice from the window. Hum, yes, risk the second train, and hope to Hennessy that Turner doesn't score a century before lunch, nor Gifford take a hat-trick. That's enough thinking about cricket for today.

John Hennessy, for many years the sports editor of *The Times*, had the reputation of being a tough egg, but barring a couple of brief explosions I always got on well with him (and even the explosions were mostly due to an intermediate character who liked making trouble). Hennessy could be hard, but he had a sense of humour, as most people do who are brought up 'in the south suburbs, at the Elephant'. I am sure he thought that some of my more eccentric efforts, such as when I reported a school's rounders match or a ladies' bowls match to the neglect of the cricket, were very midsummer madness, but he stood faithfully by me.

I was, of course, very proud to be writing for *The Times*. I had been proud to be working for the BBC, and for *The Guardian* and *The Sunday Telegraph* and a great many assorted other people over a great many assorted subjects over the years, but it was writing for *The Times* that gave me a special satisfaction. I first wrote a report for them in 1942 when Taunton played the Royal Naval College, Dartmouth. I was editor of Taunton School magazine at the time, and sent it off speculatively. I never was paid, but it went in. Thereafter I contributed with more frequency, and it was *The Times* who came to my rescue when the West of England Home Service of the BBC was wantonly closed down in 1970 (but that dismal story I have told elsewhere). I was asked some years later, when *The Times* published a cricket supplement, to write a piece about our cricket writers. It is not authoritative – there was no time to go up to London and search the archives. I had to write it from the resources of my own small library. But it came from the heart.

'Over four thousand persons visited Lord's Ground yesterday to witness one of the most remarkable spectacles that has occurred at this place for a long time past . . . The Colonials beat the greatest and most powerful club in the world by nine wickets. They were loudly cheered by the assembled multitude.' Thus *The Times* in 1878, after the Australians had beaten Marylebone in a single day. I do not know who wrote the account, but it was very likely 'Sporting Ward', so-called to distinguish him from Humphry Ward. Bernard Darwin has told us how the omniscient Ward used to cover practically all the games in the newspaper. Ward must have been a veteran by 1896, but his report of the Australians v. MCC in that year (when the Australians were out for 18) seems to me very much in the same style as the 1878 account, and we know that Ward wrote the latter. So 'Sporting Ward' has a tolerable claim to be our first cricket writer. On the other hand, sports writers in those days were not encouraged to develop an individual style. Darwin himself, who began writing about golf for the paper soon after Ward's retirement, was the pioneer.

The first cricket correspondent *per se* that *The Times* possessed was Sidney Pardon. He was acquired from *The Daily Telegraph*, and was editor of *Wisden* for 34 years, until his death in 1925. He is reported to have suffered from bad eyesight and nervous irritability, despite which he built a weighty reputation. When *Wisden* became too big a job to be combined with a full-time correspondent's work, Pardon was succeeded on the paper by A. C. M. Croome. Croome was also an acerb man, whose views became influential. An article he wrote in 1921, critical of the play of Hubert Ashton, is thought to have kept Ashton out of the England side that year, at a time when there was strong opinion in Ashton's favour (opinion strengthened in retrospect). This story is recounted by Sir Home Gordon, who adds: 'Croome had called me into the writing-room of the pavilion to read that paragraph before he sent it to the printer, and he had made at least four drafts before it satisfied his cricket conscience.' Ah! those were the days, leisurely days, when a correspondent could settle down to a succession of drafts and wrestlings with his conscience in a pavilion writing-room. Croome's life was saved once by W. G. Grace. He was playing for Gloucestershire, and chasing a ball to the boundary injured himself in the throat on a spiked railing. W.G. held the edges of the wound together for half an hour until a surgical needle could be fetched. Croome said the hand never shook, though W.G. had been fielding out for over 400 runs, and a twitch might have been fatal.

Croome died in 1930, after a long illness which had mellowed him. E. W. Swanton recalls seeing him at Old Trafford that year, a bowed figure with an unrolled umbrella looking at the team groups in the Long Room during a break for rain. Of course both he and Pardon made their contributions anonymously, as did all other sports writers in the paper, apart from very occasional and probably accidental exceptions – golf pieces can be found with the initials B.D. at their foot. I have no doubt that the high standard of sports writing in the paper was connected with the anonymity rule. I think it was Delane who said that a name at the top of a report was merely a barrier between the news and the public. Nowadays I am afraid we are too concerned with looking for a 'style', and if we find one are trapped by it.

Anonymity did not prevent a variety of interesting people from writing for us about cricket, not all of them of course holding the rank of 'cricket correspondent'. One who did, in the 'thirties, was R. B. Vincent. He was known as 'Beau' Vincent, and recalled the *Punch* cartoon of the Victorian maidservant: 'Five reporters, ma'am, and a gentleman from *The Times*.' But he had his oddities, such as carrying his dentures in his overcoat pocket. Robertson-Glasgow has written affectionately about Vincent. Once they were walking down a street in Manchester during a Test, and saw two posters side by side: one said, 'READ ROBERTSON-GLASGOW IN THE MORNING POST', and the other 'READ THE TIMES AND SEE WHAT REALLY HAPPENED': which, when you come to think of it, was another one up to anonymity.

Dudley Carew, novelist and lyricist, wrote about cricket for *The Times*. His book, *To The Wicket*, is one of the pleasantest and wittiest guides to cricket between the wars. O. L. Owen, who was for 43 years rugby correspondent, did some cricket as well. Owen was one of the old-style all-rounders, a kind of lesser C. B. Fry. He played rugby and cricket for Swansea, soccer for Bristol City, and reached a high standard in athletics, boxing and hockey. He is said to have reported a wider variety of sports than anyone who ever worked on the paper, even Sporting Ward, to say nothing of covering the last public execution in France. Geoffrey Green, though best remembered for his soccer writings, was once the cricket correspondent as well. D. J. Insole, writing in 1960, thought him the outstanding sports writer of the time, and Darwin paid him high tribute in one of his volumes of autobiography. But Green's destiny was to write about soccer, and the elongation of the soccer season made it increasingly difficult to combine the two jobs. So in 1954 John Woodcock took over the cricket.

The Sage of Longparish, as he is now affectionately known, was then a slip of a boy, 27 years old and looking about 10 years younger. A youthful appointment, a long and happy term of service – it is a pattern which has several times recurred. It is no business of mine to discuss the merits of a friend and a colleague, but in one respect at least he achieved something which none of his predecessors had done. For *The Times* decided, in 1967, that anonymity must depart. The date was

January 23. John Woodcock was in South Africa, and January 23 fell in the middle of a Test match. I suppose it was thought incongruous that 'Our Cricket Correspondent' should suddenly acquire an identity in the middle of a match. At any rate the preview, on January 20, revealed all. Johnny had asserted the primacy of cricket by beating all the others to the by-line by three days. This caused sufficient of a stir for the Sage himself to hear the news in a South African radio bulletin.

They have been a rich assortment of characters, the people who have written about cricket for *The Times* – and I have not mentioned some of the richest. There was Denzil Batchelor, for instance, who in several ways resembled Falstaff, and who happily called his autobiography 'Babbled of Green Fields'. I suppose sports writing is no more than babbling of green fields, but I think also that these men have, almost always, served the game, the paper, and the English language affectionately and responsibly. It is a tradition of which anyone who writes about cricket for *The Times* is conscious, is proud, and strives to maintain.

Cricket writers are on the whole a genial and entertaining lot, and it would be easy to go on writing about them, but I fear self-indulgent. And then who to leave out? There would always be one more. But I must say a few more words about John Arlott, to whom I have so far referred only in passing. I have told how I first met him when I was a novice at Taunton in 1948, and how helpful he was. It has always been one of his qualities to go out of his way to be generous to young men aspiring to the same trade. Indeed, even more generous than it sounds, because the amount of radio commentary – though far more was done in 1948 than today – was limited; and even if a likely newcomer only received a small slice of the cake, there was that little less for the others. But John is a very kind man. Another striking quality has been his reluctance to speak ill of any of his friends and acquaintances behind their backs. He can be sharp enough to their faces. But if you were to say to him, for instance (to take an entirely fictional character) 'I think Bloswancock is a bloody man', and Bloswancock is absent, he will immediately, though tactfully, think of something kind to say about him. I have always thought this quality is a mark of a good man: especially among cricket reporters, for though I have just spoken approvingly of them, they do tend to be terrible gossips, and touches of bitchiness are not unknown.

It is always difficult to write about an old friend. If you praise him people say 'the usual backslapping stuff', and if you are rude about him, people say 'disloyal blighter'. Once the editor of *The Cricketer* asked me for a piece to mark John's birthday (the sixty-fifth, I think it was) and stressed that he wanted a critical assessment, not an encomium. So I stiffened the sinews, summoned up the blood and did my best to be rude about John. I quote the result (it was of course only a small part of the article):

He can be garrulous, but this is often a useful quality in a radio commentator. I remember attempting commentary on the first half-hour once at Southampton. The fast bowlers were on, walking back very slowly to their marks, and four runs were scored, all in singles. It was a painful experience, both for me and the listeners. John would have sailed through it. Still, I remember a thoughtful comment from Trevor Bailey, when John was completing his biography of Trueman (an astonishing *tour de force*, done at high speed). Fred was going down to Alresford to stay with John, to survey the manuscript. Trevor, awe-stricken at the prospect, wondered 'Which of them will stop talking first?'

'I have heard John called patronizing, indeed I might at one time and another have used the word myself. While I do not think this is a just criticism, he does sometimes assume a subservience in his friends which can irritate them. No doubt he drinks too much. This failing, which we have in common, was one of the foundations of our friendship. Besides, what is a wine correspondent expected to do?

I pass to a more serious criticism. I have sometimes thought that he lacked what might be called severity in logic. I am not thinking of him now as a cricket commentator, but as a poet, and a kind of politician (he was President of the Young Liberals long before he became – to him, the greatest compliment he has been paid – President of the Cricketers' Association); and also, I suppose the word would be, as a philosopher.

Another common ground for our friendship was a belief, not entirely orthodox, in Christian truth. Among the countless radio programmes to which he has contributed was *Christian Forum*, in which I used to take the chair. His faith, I think wavered after the death of his eldest son in a road accident. How could a loving God permit this kind of thing to happen? This was a human reaction, but he knew his Christian apologetic, knew that the world was full of such miseries. This is an illustration of what I mean by a lack of severity in logic. So was his insistence thereafter in wearing a black tie almost every day, year after year after year. This went beyond a proper Christian mourning, and became perilously near a pagan rite, like Queen Victoria having Albert's dinner clothes, down to the studs, freshly laid out every night, for nearly 40 years.

John's hymns, three of which appear in *The BBC Hymn-Book*, are concerned with praying about the weather, an activity with many distinguished precedents, but again not a strictly logical one. Another illustration: at the time of the controversy about the proposed South African tour in 1970, he did dither a bit, when many of his colleagues and friends were looking to him for a strong lead.

But these things are no more than the defects of his qualities, and it is easier to dwell on the qualities. In *Sort of a Cricket Person*, his first volume of autobiography, Jim Swanton wrote this in a discussion of cricket commentators through the years:

All these experienced men have their individual virtues and their particular admirers, but to one cricket owes a special debt, not so much because he happens to have done more talking about the game over the last quarter of a century than anyone else, but because in the post-war years his manner and style attracted a new and wider audience. I mean, of course, John Arlott who managed to weave together as much information about the progress of the game as the average listener wanted, along with the fruits of his observation on players, spectators and the scene generally, all laced with humour and put across in an intimate, confidential way and a rich Hampshire accent. The voice evoked the village green and rustic England and leisurely days in the sun.

In their first few years together as commentators, John and Jim did not always get on too well. I reveal no secrets in saying this. They came from very different backgrounds. John wrote some verses about Jim which began

> *O stately is my manner,*
> *And Swanton is my name,*
> *And in* The Daily Telegraph
> *I write about THE GAME*

I refrain from quoting the rest of it, partly because I am not sure I can remember it, partly because I do not wish to stir old embers: it was a naughty but witty lampoon. The two men were far too intelligent, and came to respect each other too much, to let a feud develop.

I would add a paragraph to Jim's assessment of John as a radio commentator. Because John had this beguiling gift of words and an eye for the unusual incident, some austere cricketers tended to think of him as no more than a phrase-maker. His phrase-making was only a secondary attribute. He worked very hard at learning his craft. When he was beginning just after the war, the Hampshire side used sometimes to grow tired of his incessant questions. 'Yes', he would say, after they had briefly described some new bowler as a 'legger' or a 'seamer', 'yes, but what does he *do*? What is his dangerous ball? Can he flight it?' and so on and on. In this way he acquired, and continued to acquire, a vast amount of knowledge about what goes on in the first-class game. Yet he has always been known among first-class cricketers as a man who does not betray confidences – which is why he receives so many.

Of Arlott the policeman, Arlott the wine expert, Arlott the collector of antiques, I am not qualified to write. Arlott the poet was thought one of the brightest prospects of his youthful time, but he did not persevere with it. I have asked him why, and he usually says, with a wry, not to say gnomic, shrug: 'The words stopped coming.' I expect he simply had too much to do. Poetry is time consuming. Despite his staggering capacity for work, he had to make his way in a variety of highly competitive fields, and he had increasingly little opportunity for 'emotion recollected in tranquillity', though he still attains it from time to time in his prose.

Has he been a happy man? His life has been scarred by more than one tragedy. I expect that he has had times of intense happiness, such as can only be experienced by one who has also had intensely *un*happy times. This is an illustration of the truth that the best things are only won through suffering. But, in good times and bad, he has continued to be a source of happiness to a great many.

Partly because of his sense of fun. I have heard it said of his broadcast commentaries that he must have 'thought up the jokes beforehand'. He may have done this occasionally, but he has never needed to 'think them up'. When Tufty Mann, the South African spinner, was giving George Mann, the English captain, a terrible time, and John decided it was a bad case of 'Mann's inhumanity to Mann', he can hardly have foreseen such a situation arising. The situation produced the words. And once I was in the box at a Test at Trent Bridge at the beginning of the day's play, Trevor Bailey began at 11.25 with a statement of the position of the game and a few minutes later said, 'Here come the umpires, wearing their new short coats, looking rather like dentists. Over to John Arlott.' John immediately replied, 'It occurs to me, Trevor, that it is rather suitable for the umpires to look like dentists, since it is one of their duties to draw stumps.'

XIII
Envoi

'Times go by turns, and chances change by course,
From foul to fair, from better hap to worse'
Southwell

The Sage of Longparish says of our reports in *The Times*, 'I write
about the cricket, and Alan writes about "A Day at the Cricket"',
and this is a perceptive remark. I hope to write about a few more
days at the cricket before it is time to draw stumps: but my own day
has at best reached a late tea interval. Indeed, most of this book is
about the play before lunch, rather like a *Sunday Times* report.
I am not very optimistic about the evening session. There are too
many things I dislike about modern cricket – the excess of
bouncers, the disappearance of leg-spin, the commercialism, the
Sunday bashes, the plague of hysterical appeals. I do not expect to
enjoy the game as I have done in the past. I do not mind so much
when it rains. Sometimes I am glad of the chance to escape from a
dull match to the bar, especially at Bristol when the Glorious
Redheaded Imperturbable Pamela (known by the acronym of
GRIP) is presiding. But the game still has its moments, and I look
forward to a few more yet.

How important is cricket? It has been important to me because it
has helped me to earn a living. But how seriously should we care
about it? The best of games, yes, it is still that, at least for those who
have taken to it and respect it (not 'love' it. I distrust anyone who
says he 'loves' cricket). The best sports writers, and not only about
cricket, are those who have interests in other areas, and can
therefore keep a sense of proportion.

Is cricket, for instance, worth praying about? Or to put it another
way, is it a fit subject for prayer? Once P. F. Warner was taking a

cricket team to Australia, and asked a bishop travelling by the same boat whether it was permissible to pray for victory. The bishop said that 'anything which conduces to the glory of England' was a proper subject for prayer, and Warner undertook that his petitions would be regular and devoted. He won the rubber, so the thesis was at least not disproved, though I do not recall, when it came to offering thanks and praise at the end of the tour, that he included any but temporal members of his team.

It is an old question this praying for sporting success, and it contains much the same traps and illogicalities as praying for success in war, especially when the other side is doing the same, with the same sincerity and to the same God. (The battle of Dunbar in 1650 is the classic example: the Scots were so confident that God was on their side that they weeded out from their Army any men suspected of leading immoral lives, including some of their best warriors. Cromwell was so worried about fighting fellow-Christians that he wrote to the Scottish ministers, 'I beseech you, in the bowels of Christ, think it possible you may be mistaken'. The English won, less for the efficacy of their prayers, one feels, than because Cromwell was the better general). You have the same problem in praying about the weather, when two equally earnest worshippers may want quite different sorts of weather. But I am not going to be drawn into the theology of the matter.

Even if it is foolish to pray about cricket, there is no doubt that many of us succumb, especially when we are young. Sir Neville Cardus has told us how, a Lancashire boy at Old Trafford, he would pray that Mold would bowl out Ranjitsinhji with the third ball of the next over, middle stump. He felt that by specifying both the middle of the over and the middle stump, he was giving the Almighty a reasonable margin of error. Myself, in youth, I was firmly discouraged from praying about sporting encounters, but I do remember cheating occasionally. There was that Cup Final between Newcastle United and Arsenal. It was in 1932 when I was eight, and I am not sure why I felt so passionately about that particular match. But I have the clearest recollection of how, after I had punctiliously and audibly completed my regular prayers, and mother had said goodnight and switched out the light, I would dive under the bedclothes and add a secret, urgent postscript on behalf of Newcastle.

This turned out to be one of the Lord's more spectacular triumphs, for not only did Newcastle win, but did so by a disputed goal when, or so every infuriated Arsenal supporter maintained, the referee had momentarily been struck blind.

What cricketer, at all levels of the game, has not uttered some kind of prayer when he has seen a high catch coming towards him in the deep? Albert Knight of Leicestershire and England, was, so far as I know, the only one in the first-class game who, the ball safely caught, would pay public acknowledgements to his Maker, bowing his head and even, if it had been a particularly hard one, bending his knee. I thought of Knight when David Sheppard, on a tour of Australia when nothing had been going right with his fielding, at last caught one. He did not bow the head, but ran round in a happy little circle of thanksgiving, throwing himself catches. He was interrupted by a bellow from his captain, Dexter. It had been a no-ball and the batsmen were still running.

Knight would also pause to pray when beginning his innings, as automatically as taking guard. That explosive Lancashire fast bowler Walter Brearley, when he realised what was going on, threatened to report him to MCC. Sir Neville recalls the incident in his preface to *Hit Hard and Enjoy It* by T. C. Dodds which was published in 1976. It was probably the last piece of prose Neville wrote, and it graced a thought-provoking and amusing book. I have known Carter Dodds (he was called by cricketers, with their gift for feeble and unsuitable nicknames, 'Dickie') for a long time; knew him, indeed, when he was beginning his first-class career with Essex just after the war, and remember very well talking with him in those days on the subject of prayer and its relationship to daily life, including cricket. I can therefore vouch – not that it needs vouching for – that the views he sets out in his book are not in any way coloured by his subsequent success. I am sure that had he been a failure as a cricketer his faith would have been unchanged.

The cases of Knight and Dodds are not on all fours. Knight's was a simple, evangelical faith. 'If ye shall ask any thing in my name, I will do it': so why not a hundred runs? Dodds is a supporter of the Moral Re-Armament movement (to which he gave the proceeds of his benefit) and MRA take a slightly more sophisticated view of prayer. I am not going to discuss its merits as a movement – I am not a supporter of it myself, though I have had many friends who have been. For them prayer or 'guidance' as it is more commonly called, is a two-way communication with God. You have a 'quiet time' in which you put your problems to him, and you note with pen and paper if possible what thoughts he puts into your mind in reply. You are not *asking* for anything, except advice.

Now this, always assuming that you believe in a personal and loving God, is a sensible way of praying. Thus Dodds did not pray that he might score a century. He asked God, 'How do you want me to play cricket?' And the answer came: 'Hit the ball hard and enjoy it.' It took some time, as he honestly records, before he had the courage to carry out God's instructions. When he did, he was transformed from one of the slowest opening batsmen in the country to one of the fastest, overnight, which made Frank Rist, the Essex coach, call him 'the miracle man'.

When he took his benefit match (the match was the most important thing in a cricketer's benefit in those days) he wondered whether to insure against the weather. His guidance was not to insure because God had said: 'If I want you to have the money, you shall have it.' He accepted this and the weather cleared at the last minute, Compton scored a century before lunch, and the benefit was a huge success. He then asked what he should do with the money, and God answered, if I may risk an august paraphrase, 'Give it away': which he did.

This may not tell you a great deal about God, but it tells you all you need to know, and admire, about Dodds. He has the quality of the saints.

The trouble with this kind of praying is that it can degenerate into superstition. Dodds had, according to his own account, already several clear indications from God that he should marry a girl called Ann, with whom he was not in love. This is his description of the decisive moment:

We were playing Somerset at Valentine's (!) Park in Ilford. It was a hot day, and two Somerset batsmen were set, and were despatching our bowling to all parts of the field. In the middle of the afternoon Bill Greensmith was bowling his leg-breaks, and just as his arm was coming over for one delivery the thought popped into my mind that if a wicket fell to that ball, then Ann was definitely the girl I was meant to marry.

To my consternation I saw the ball was one of those that all leg-break bowlers deliver occasionally. The ball slipped out of his fingers and bounced halfway down the wicket. The batsman could have hit it to any part of the field. Instead he hit it straight at me and I caught him out!

This is no good at all. It is entirely pagan, like examining the entrails or touching wood, or touching the peak of your cap before the bowler delivers. It reduces God to a hazard and all the other cricketers concerned to automata. If God wants to ensure a happy marriage, he has better ways of doing it than making the ball slip out of Greensmith's fingers. We can all understand what made the incident so vivid to Dodds at that time, but it spoils his argument, and does no justice to his faith.

To return to my original point: is it any good praying that you might make a hundred runs when you next go in to bat, or about the steepler coming to you at long-off, or even that you may hit the ball hard and enjoy it – for some of us are not given the requisite talents? I quote to you a few lines from Leslie Weatherhead, as saintly a man as Dodds, which he made in the course of an address concerned with whether it was worth praying about the weather. He said, bluntly, that he did not think it was ('Take an umbrella and grin!') but he added

> I am sure a man can be as good a Christian who believes in praying about the weather, as a man who does not. And if bad weather makes you pray when good weather would leave you prayerless, it could be argued that it is a good thing to pray, whatever you pray about. It is a good thing for a child to talk to his father about *anything* that worries him.

One way or another, then, those prayers of Warner and Knight and Dodds and you and me: they may not have been wasted after all.

I remember a day at the Oval when an English batsman was injured, and the physiotherapist rushed out to attend him. It seemed to me that he was administering a pain-killing injection. Trevor Bailey by my side said, 'No, I think it's a spray.' John Arlott standing behind us for he had just vacated the commentator's seat, leant forward and said, 'No, not too bad, I think. Not past spraying for.'

Cricket is still worth a spray of hope, and even, by Weatherhead's slim thread of logic, a prayer. I think I shall risk a private petition to the Lord, not for a hundred runs, not for a Yorkshire championship, for my native county, though still dear to me, seems determined to make its land (I write in 1984) 'desolate, and an hissing; every one that passeth thereby shall be astonished and hiss because of all the plagues thereof'. Yea, they will even wag their heads at the county which men once called the perfection of beauty. I am afraid I am a Jeremiah now as far as Yorkshire cricket is concerned.

But I repeat, cricket is worth a prayer. I call upon Jim Swanton and John Woodcook to join in. Jim is a High Churchman, so high that he reminded me of the slight transliteration of Montgomery's hymn, 'For ever with the Lord', which ends, you remember, very nearly

> *And nightly pitch my moving tent*
> *A day's march nearer Rome*

though he still clings to the Pusey bank. Johnny is patron of the church of Longparish, where he valiantly clings to the 1662 liturgy, and has promised that one day I may preach, miserable Baptist though I am. So between us we will make quite an ecumenical trio of petitioners, and my suggestion is that we don't worry the Lord with everything at once, but just put in a word for fewer bouncers and more leg-spinners. There is a lot more to say of course, but Cardus was sensible in concentrating on the middle stump in the middle of the over.

Whether the prayer is answered or not, I will still give thanks to the Giver of all Good for countless happy days at the cricket, the game with which I grew up.